A TRANQUIL MIND

A TRANQUIL MIND

A BEDSIDE BOOK OF PHILOSOPHY

C. WHITAKER-WILSON

SKEFFINGTON AND SON LTD
FOUNDED 1858

London   New York   Melbourne   Sydney   Cape Town

CONTENTS

TO HER

whose sweet and loving companionship has transformed my home into a haven of contentment and peace- and in recognition of the great part she played in the general outlining of this book—

TO MY BELOVED WIFE

RUBY

I gratefully dedicate the completed volume

PREFACE

PEACE of Mind is no primary principle in philosophy. It is an attainment in life to be striven for, the actual contemplation of it being a study of the Superiority Complex.

The word *mind* is a collective term that includes *all* our senses, our faculties, our complexes, *as directed by the brain*. Because of this it is impossible to make a study of tranquillity as an attainment in life without going back to first principles.

.In the earlier chapters of this book you will find I have gone into most aspects of thinking; you will also find I have offered you an experiment in time well worth your while to make - at least, if not, your experience will be different from what mine has been.

I ask you to study the Prologue closely and to accept my definition of the soul of man —or, at all events, to believe in its function as I have described it. Then, in the later chapters, you will find I shall lead you into a study of the Superiority Complex which alone can give you a tranquil mind. It will come to you in the reading as it has again come to me in the writing but, *if it is to stay*, some amount of persistence on your part will be necessary where the experiment is concerned.

May I say at once that, as an expression, 'Superiority Complex' is seldom used and entirely misunderstood when it is? Far too many people imagine that he who has the Superiority Complex thinks no end of himself and looks down his nose at other people. That is, actually, one of the worst forms of the Inferiority Complex, if they did but know it.

The Complex Superior is a direct tendency ('complex' means *tendency of mind* as used here) towards the attainment of a powerful mind and a humble heart. If you have r'ready attained it you must be gentle and virile at the same time.

At all events the study of that complex - together with some thought of the Complex Supreme—is what this book is all about ; if you read it carefully you will find yourself *thinking about thinking.*

That you will make the experiment I am quite sure; but I hope you will regard this book, once you have read it, as a *bedside* book. I say that because I know the value of quiet reading before sleep—and, remember, this book is called *A Tranquil Mind.*

If making the experiment changes your whole outlook on life I shall not be in the least surprised indeed, I *cannot* be, because I know what it has done for me; but if doubt assails you on the question of life *here* and life *hereafter*, I humbly suggest you read the Epilogue more than once.

The thought reminds me that I am now writing my Preface and that I have an acknowledgment to make because I have quoted several passages from Maurice Maeterlinck's fairy play *The Blue Bird.* The translation I have used is published by Methuen who, incidentally, published four out of my five books on London.

C. WHITAKER-WILSON

The Walnut Orchard, Chorleywood Common, Hertfordshire.

PROLOGUE: THE SOUL OF MAN

EVER since man first found himself in this world of ours he has been wondering whether or not he really possesses a soul and, if so, whether he has discovered exactly what it is. Quite early in the world's life man definitely made up his mind on the point: all things in nature, according to his findings, were endowed with souls. He was quite sure about the animals, even if a little less sure about the plants. About himself he was apparently in no doubt: his instincts seemed to tell him he was the possessor of what he thought must be a soul.

That it was immortal never occurred to him. Plato first put forward that idea; it must have startled his contemporaries.

Plato held that the soul was temporarily connected with the body which it survived at death. Aristotle's thinking went a little further: he believed there were three distinct kinds of soul. The nutrient soul, in his view, was responsible for vitalizing everything in the plant world; the sentient soul accounted for the instinct in animals; the thinking soul, which man alone possessed, accounted for everything connected with human development. In that last thought the good Aristotle came very near the truth.

In the Middle Ages these theories underwent considerable modification—but that was merely to reconcile them with the tenets of Christianity. In this there is nothing very surprising; but Descartes struck a somewhat novel note in saying '*Cogito, ergo sum*— I think, therefore I am.' He said he was certain that the soul and the body were two separate beings. He went on to declare that some Perfect Being must exist, arguing that if no such Being existed he (Aristotle) would never have even thought of Him. 'My mind', said Aristotle, 'is finite. Everything about me is finite. Therefore a Being who implanted in my mind the idea of His existence *must be infinite.*'

A simple deduction if ever there was one; but we can hardly miss the fact that Aristotle doubted his own immortality.

There have been others. John Locke, as an example, considered the soul of man to be his mind which he likened to a sheet of blank paper ready to record impressions. Experience, and that alone, was the source of everything worth while in us.

To read Leibniz, or Spinoza, or Hume, or Mill, is to find their views so conflicting that there is little chance of forming a clear idea as to whether the soul of man is sufficiently important to trouble one's head about. These philosophers cannot all be right even if they are not all wrong. And yet one feels one *must* have an answer.

The more one thinks the more satisfactory seems the theory that man does possess a soul which survives him at death, and it becomes increasingly difficult to understand why Christ spent so much time explaining to his audiences what they were to expect if it were not a fact that we are immortal.

In order to discover exactly what the soul of man is hurls no-one into philosophy of the deeper kind; the question can be answered quite simply, and the truth arrived at, by following out a very ordinary line of elimination.

The first thought may well be the *brain*: is the soul of man his brain? It is not a bad idea to look at an illustrated encyclopedia or a medical treatise. A picture of the brain is not exactly impressive; it looks disgustingly like lamb's sweetbread-- but *everything is known* about the brain. Medical science has divided it up into five main parts, and the scientists have discovered exactly what is the function of each of them.

The medulla, for instance, begins at the base of the skull; it is about an inch in length and nerve-cell stations of the greatest importance are secreted in it. One of these controls the breathing mechanism. Above the medulla is the bridge connecting it with the mid-brain. Other parts are the cerebrum and the cerebellum. Any reliable writer can describe how various parts of the brain act upon vision, hearing, touch, and smell—all of which makes fascinating reading; but no-one has attempted to describe how man *thinks* with his brain even though the action of thoughts has to some extent been traced.

The brain of man has been measured; it has been weighed; it has been photographed. That alone is enough to cause us to reject the idea that the soul of man is his brain. It is a little disconcerting to think one's soul is so many inches long and so many thick, that it weighs something like three pounds, and that there is nothing in the appearance of it to excite one's admiration. The soul, one would hope, must make a lovely picture.

Another thought is the *mind*. Is the soul of man his mind? This certainly sounds more feasible, but only until one remembers that the mind is merely a collective term which includes *all* our senses and that these same senses are just the normal functions of the entire nervous system *as directed by the brain*. We all imagine we are stylists of a sort; the mind is directly responsible for our particular and individual style. As the brain is in command of the nervous system, and as the mind is just a *term for all our senses*, the mind will not do for an answer.

The truth is only to be come by as a result of going back to the beginning of everything connected with us. For the reasons given, it cannot be the mind and is still less likely to be the physical brain or, if it is, there is no question of its being immortal.

No; the answer is that the soul of man is his *power to think*. Just that and only that—the *power* to think, not the thinking machine itself.

Admittedly, such a definition makes it difficult to account for the total imbecile who, seemingly, is denied the power to think. None of us would deny the poor idiot a soul. That goes without saying, but we have to remember that the Creator has permitted the existence of every imaginable distortion of Man Beautiful even to the degradation of Siamese twins. Thus it comes about that certain human entities have been allowed to go through life here with their souls apparently out of commission. We can only hope— indeed, we assume— that the deficiency will be made up to them hereafter. Less than that is inconceivable.

The next point of interest is: *when exactly does the soul strike the body?* The word 'strike' is used advisedly because the soul is not 'just born' within us; it does not come along when we come along, so to speak.

At the best, birth is a slow process. Most of us seem to take our time getting here. The soul is not born within us in the same slow and laborious manner, taking longer in some instances than in others. The brain and mind do develop gradually—that is a known and rather an obvious fact—but the soul comes at a *given second* in time. It is the direct result of a flash, a throb on the ether.

Man himself comes from a germ. He may be expelled from his mother in an incomplete state and may not even be considered to have lived at all. When that happens he can be only said to exist as mass and matter. He has no sense—he has no *hope* of sense—about him; but once the *quickening* has taken place he is equipped for his life on earth even if he does not live long enough to make use of his equipment. His quickening means that Almighty God has been pleased to strike yet another human entity with an immortal soul.

That is when the soul strikes the body: at the quickening *And within the hour the mother knows it.*

It is the very existence of a soul within us that constitutes the main difference between us and the lower animals, who have no souls.

Among people who possess pets they love, this statement may not be particularly welcome; but any theory suggesting that animals possess souls will not stand up to even the most elementary test. By the laws of nature it is impossible that if one animal has a soul another has not. If one animal possesses a soul the entire animal world must possess souls.

Many of us own attractive dogs whom we love and who love us. We are apt to declare that our dog understands everything we say to him. Probably he does; but what do we do when he contracts an incurable disease, when he is seriously injured, or even when he reaches an age that renders life a misery? In our very humanity we have him (as we say) 'put to sleep'.

Supposing something of the kind happens to our own mother, whom we love and who loves us, and who also understands everything we say to her? Do we have her 'put to sleep' in the same way? The answer is that we do *not* have that done. She has a soul; it is murder to take the life of a creature who has a soul.

If animals really have souls we are not within our right if we destroy any one of them —not even those we dislike most. We may not kill a slug, although it will eat our best green vegetables and most of our white lupins; we may not kill a fly even though we know it to be a pestilential germ-carrier; we must never destroy a wasp, nor even a 'flea that is, *if we believe* animals have souls. As for a national rat-week, we should denounce it as a horrifying pogrom.

It is useless for us to argue that pets are not pests. They certainly are not, but where are we going to draw the line? Who are *we* to say which animal has a soul and which has not and how are we going to *prove* our contentions, anyway? Where is our authority for permitting the destruction of any animal —even of our own pet who has been run over and has had his back broken?

Furthermore, we must not countenance the killing of an animal for use as food. We must not forget that if our charming little puppy has a soul we can hardly deny one to an equally charming little lamb who frolics innocently in the meadow.

In any case, should we still be in doubt, we have to remember that Christ, who loved all creatures, once deliberately caused the destruction of a herd of swine.

It has been said that we ourselves are descended from the apes. The truth is more likely to be that we are developed from some type of anthropoid family. It certainly does not strain the imagination to reconstruct a certain scene in the early stages of this world's life. It is not difficult to suppose that the Creator, having watched —through the centuries —the gradual development of (perhaps, ape-like) creatures, said: 'To these two I will give immortal souls. Henceforth man shall be blessed with the power to think.

Such power shall guide him through his earthly life. It alone shall survive his physical death on earth.'

Whether or not the two were actually Adam and Eve hardly matters.

The next point is easily answered. *When does the soul leave the body?*

Obviously, at the point of death. That establishes the fact that the soul leaves the body *at a given second in time.* A man may be dying on the last night of a year. He may still be breathing at 11.59 p.m. He may not even have breathed his last breath at 59 minutes, 58 seconds past the hour of eleven. If he dies at the 59th second he dies in the old year; if he lives one second longer he dies at the beginning of a new year, so fine a point may be put upon his going.

The very fact that we all die at a given second in our reckoning of time makes *death* the logical complement to the *quickening.* It is *not* the logical complement to birth. That is why God may be said to strike each human entity with its immortal soul *at a given instant* in time. From that moment, until the moment of death, the body houses the soul which itself does not grow like the brain or the hair. When it comes it comes as a flash on the ether; it comes at the quickening; it leaves at death.

Where the soul goes to at the point of death was described by Christ, but nothing was said as to how it reaches its destination.

The omission was probably intentional. Christ's disciples, and audiences generally, were not scientifically-minded. Since those early days man has had the best part of two thousand years for purposes of research; he has gained much knowledge. With less opportunities than he has actually had he would have realized (sooner or later) that God made the laws of nature and, having made them, *went so far as to obey them.*

The account of the creation, as given in Genesis, is a very simple story. The writer used the simplest words he could think of. 'And God saw that it was good' is a phrase he made repeated use of. In other words, he pointed out that God made what we call 'nature' *and made an excellent set of laws to keep it going.*

So that, because everything connected with us follows some law of nature, there is a definite *technique* regarding our translation at death. We had to wait a very long time—actually until only a few years ago—before the Creator was good enough to reveal one of His more 'advanced' secrets to man on earth: *it was when He allowed man to make use of the ether as well as of the air and to understand the principles of what we now call radio transmission.*

To any serious student of the New Testament it is obvious that Christ was able to communicate with his Father whenever he chose. Even to that there was a technique—merely because nothing happens in this world (or out of it) except by the operation of one or other of the laws of nature. The fact is: the Son of God possessed what may be said to *correspond* to a radio transmitting and receiving set; and, by what he himself would have probably regarded as his ordinary process of thinking, he was able to make (and keep in) continuous contact with the Throne of Grace.

He became aware of it as a child; because he made continual use of it he was able to say with perfect truth that he and his Father were one. On one occasion only—so far as we know—was that ethereal line of communication what we should call 'out of order': it was during the three hours on the cross. The Son must indeed have felt himself to be cut off from the Father and his friends alike, hanging there 'twixt earth and heaven. He had already transmitted: '*Father, forgive them.*' . . . Now there was silence in his soul: no message could be transmitted; none was received. The next moment he complained of it: '*My God, my God, why hast thou forsaken me?*'

Admitting that Christ's case was exceptional, and that he was able to transmit and receive messages at will, the fact remains that it was he who taught men to pray—at least, it was he who assured them their prayers would be heard. But, again, nothing was said about the technique of all this, about the action of natural laws making such contacts possible. Not surprising; it would not have been understood in those far-off days.

It can, however, be understood now.

Radio transmission, in these modern days, is a very ordinary affair. If two people are holding conversation in a room, the sound of their voices travels on the air at the somewhat leisurely speed of 1125 feet a second. That is, at least, fairly accurate.

If a man takes part in a broadcast transmission, the sound of his voice *in the studio* travels, roughly, at th..t speed —and it *still* travels on the air. Once the sound of his voice passes through the microphone it ceases to be a matter for the air at all; it becomes a question of electrical variations and travels on the ether, not the air. The speed it now assumes is indeed amazing. That speed is 186,000 *miles* (not feet, mark you!) every second. In other words, fast enough to go round the world in *one-seventh of a second*. (Practically instantaneous.)

So that if a music-lover is seated in the Albert Hall, listening to a concert, and another music-lover is listening to the same programme (broadcast) in Australia, he actually hears every sound before the man in the hall.

Such facts are mere commonplaces in these days of advanced science; we think very little of them. Yet, ordinary as we have come to regard them, it is from these facts we may safely conclude that, while our conversations are vibrations on the air and moving at a comparatively slow speed, our unspoken thoughts are *vibrations on the ether*, capable of travelling at the speed of light—or even (for all we know to the contrary) much faster than that.

The next thought is grander still: by a throb on the ether we can transmit our thoughts from this world into the next. Conversely, thoughts from that world can reach us in this. More thrilling still is to know that, when our thinking here is done, *it is our actual power to think* which leaves our bodies behind and goes on by the same—or, at least, by similar—means. That is a thought worth the thinking.

Perhaps it was unfortunate that St Paul said we brought nothing into this world and took nothing out of it. He may have meant nothing *in the material sense*. If he did mean that, all well and good; but there is nothing in the Greek to suggest he meant it that way. If he meant his statement to be read and taken literally—namely, that we brought nothing and shall take nothing, material or immaterial—then, with all due respect, one is bound to contradict him.

Of all God's grand laws, that of heredity is the grandest. Also it is one of the most powerful of any directly affecting us humans. We *do* bring something with us: we bring hereditary powers, gifts, tendencies, and even weaknesses. We certainly do take plenty away with us: we take away the sum-total of our usage of those gifts and tendencies.

In other words, we take away our *experience*.

Anything less than that is inconceivable. Otherwise, what is the good of a life spent here in striving after high principles? What is the good of a life of close study and intensive reading? What is the good of filching hours from our sleep in order to gain more technique in something worth while? What is the good—of *anything*?

Such a thought means we must enter the next life with nothing in the way of credentials. Despite the fact that a man may have slogged and slaved away all his life for the sake of others, while his brother may have done just the opposite and have lived a life of sloth and idleness, if *neither* of them is to take away anything with him neither can even *hope* to be 'the good and faithful servant'.

The whole thought of immortality in relation to life here is so *immense*. We are bound to conclude that time spent in gaining technique here is time saved hereafter. If you spend your life here in the quest of knowledge and scholarship (to say nothing of the beautifying of your character) and I rot mine away drinking and gambling, can you believe we shall both arrive there on an equality?

Perhaps our best plan is to regard St Paul as writing in the first century with more enthusiasm than scientific knowledge, and to think that if he were here to be questioned now he would modify much of what he wrote then. He would certainly modify what he wrote about our lying insensate in our graves until the sound of the Last Trumpet. If Adam actually was the first conscious man, he has lain a long time in Mesopotamia—much longer than some of your friends, and mine, killed in the first great war.

Yet the Church, according to its burial service, still clings to what St Paul said. The suggestion that we shall rise at the so-called Last Day *with our bodies* will hardly stand up to examination. That is, quite apart from the thought of what cremation does to them. Waiting—possibly for millions of years—seems a poor ending to the best of what any of us try to do here. If judgement there be—and there seems no valid argument against it—surely it must be a private affair taking place upon, or soon after, arrival?

Spiritualism, as a cult, is not to everyone's liking. You yourself may not be a spiritualist. For that matter, neither am I. Whether you are one or not, you will not mind my saying that we can all afford to regard the spiritualists as having, between them, proved one thing if only one: namely, that there *is* survival after death and that it is going on *now*.

That is conceding very little to those engaged in psychical research, but if you and I cannot concede any more we can at least withhold our further belief with all due deference to those who think differently.

The reason St Paul wrote in the way he did *may* be that he was not present at the crucifixion. If he had been, he would certainly have thought differently—especially if he had heard Christ promise the penitent thief that he would be with him in Paradise 'today', not a million years hence.

It is time the Church revised the burial services on this point.

As to the spiritual body each of us receives on entry into the planes of the Eternal, it will be immortal—and because of that it will be immune from distress and disease. That we may bear at least some resemblance to our earthly appearance seems likely, if only because Christ was recognized by those who saw him after the resurrection.

An interesting point about the resurrection of Jesus is: it is the one clear instance of an earthly body being *united* to a spiritual body. On the other hand, there is nothing in the least surprising about the resurrection or the ascension: both formed a perfect complement to an unusual birth.

Rising from the dead in that way is not our prerogative.

All we can do—or, rather, get done for us —is the translation of our power to think *after* we have done all our
thinking and our bodies have become cold and inanimate,
or only exist as ashes.

Yes; the soul of man is his power to think. It strikes his
body at the quickening and leaves it at death. Possession of
such a power to think turns the act of thinking *into a power*.

That is what this part of my book is all about. The power
to think is the greatest power within us. So powerful are
our thoughts that, when we have finished our thinking
here, the power which brought our very thoughts to life
is all that survives. Everything else dies.

'It is a grand thought—but it does lay heavy stress on the
importance of thinking.

I

THE IMPORTANCE OF THINKING

SOME years ago I was walking along a seashore with a
friend. We passed a woman with her small son, both of
whom were obviously tired; the child was crying. The
woman suddenly gave the child a swinging clout across the
head in a fashion calculated to deprive him of his gumption.
We were somewhat taken aback; but it was what she said to
him that surprised us more:

'Nah, then! You *enjoy* yerself. If yer don't, I'll *make* yer!'

From which we concluded that her philosophy embraced
a theory that happiness is only attainable by compulsion.
Such philosophy was beyond me at the time, and has been
so since; yet happiness is the greatest quest of the human
race. No-one can ever deny that.

Nor should we be expected to. Unhappiness is a negative
condition of life—one into which none of us was ever
really called. The fact that we are unhappy at any given
moment, or in any given period of time, may not be our
own fault; but if it is literally true that any of us is mostly
miserable, and rarely contented, there is something the
matter with our philosophy.

Happiness is a condition of mind. Such a condition can hardly be ours every day and all day because, if it were, we should have to be both blind and deaf to the sufferings of others. It is possible to be oblivious of, and indifferent to, the sufferings of other people because selfishness can assume such proportions that life here can be lived, as it were, within a walled garden. So long as everything in that garden is lovely to one's own way of thinking, it is possible (at least, in some senses) to find happiness there. Whether or not such happiness, even when attainable, is worthy of attainment would appear doubtful; its value must be questionable even if it *seems* to be what one is really seeking.

The fact is: in order to arrive at the required state of mind for happiness one has to do some intensive thinking. The importance of thinking can never be estimated, much less overstated; so important is good and deep thinking that real health of body—which rarely comes except as a result of health of mind—is unattainable without it.

It is wholly a question of attitude of mind—in other words, of the sum-total of one's individual thoughts.

Attitude of mind *is* that, and it lays terrific emphasis on the importance of thinking. Moreover, because our attitude of mind is largely made up of our thoughts about others, any attempt to *assess* it must begin with some sort of general review of our thoughts regarding those with whom we come into contact—especially, of course, regarding people whose own attitude may prove to be in some degree irritating. People do irritate one but, for all that, philosophy does not teach us to poison our own thoughts where they are concerned. Heaven knows it is easy enough to set up *that* kind of poisoning!

It is one thing to find one's self in a blaze of wrath because of something said by someone else—it may happen any moment—but it is quite another to allow the remembrance of it to remain. Once we do that we begin to harbour resentment. If that goes on for any length of time resentment turns into a mild form of hatred. If *that* is allowed to continue it soon develops into thoughts of revenge. And revenge-in-the-mind is a form of local poisoning not always easy to deal with. The fact that we may have pleasant enough thoughts toward others (who have *not* roused our indignation) may be enough to save our minds from *general* poisoning—indeed, it *will* be enough—but there is still the local infection to deal with.

Being angry, with just and sufficient cause, is not harmful. Any philosopher will say that; but anger has to be regarded as an *abnormal* state of mind. Otherwise it is quite possible to weaken one's defences.

As an abnormality, it has to be counteracted by bringing up forces of a different nature, such as readiness to excuse faults in others. If anger (regarded as a mental condition) is allowed to develop unchecked, by very ordinary laws controlling the emotions it becomes more and more natural to be in a state of anger; the result is that it becomes increasingly easy to be more and more angry with less and less cause until the state is reached when one is literally the victim of one's own particular form of persecution.

With the mind in that state happiness is impossible. 'Fullness of living' is nothing but a meaningless phrase. Resentment is a poor bedfellow at the best of times; lying down at night harbouring thoughts of anger and ill-will merely damages the spirit. Unfortunately, the trouble does not stop there: someone else's spirit is damaged at the same time. Thoughts are powerful agencies.

Harbouring resentment atrophies all hope of forgiveness. How often has a man said: 'I can forgive him for this, even for that; but there is one thing I can *never* forgive.' And he usually proceeds to name it.

The way he puts it certainly does make it sound pretty bad. No wonder he feels like that about it! Yet, by his attitude, he is the loser all the time. His unforgiveness is acting like a festering sore. He cannot even think about the other person without a change coming over him; the very mention of his name, much less the sight of him, lashes like a whip. Whatever the justification for such anger, that man continues to be the loser. He probably suffers far more than the man who made him angry suffers. Even if he does not, he is at fault in the philosophical sense because he has allowed his balance of mind to be seriously disturbed. He would have done better to banish every thought of resentment—even if he had little or nothing in the way of actual forgiveness to substitute.

It is only the most fortunate of us who can say we are never disturbed to anger; but it is indeed a misfortune when any one of us comes to the decision that the only course we can pursue is (as we say) to *get even* with someone else, to make him suffer at least as much as we have suffered. Resentment so deep as to disturb us to action of that kind is an *abrasive*. There is no philosophy that teaches anything to the contrary; but if we are determined to 'get even' with someone else for an insult, or an injury done, we are usually ready to risk what there is to risk and prepare to go ahead.

Having thus thrown philosophy to the four winds, we proceed with our plainest basic English. We have been hurt, and we intend to hurt in reply. We forget that resentment *is* an abrasive and that we shall return from the fray not a little damaged in mind. We *must* put the other fellow in his place, no matter at what cost to us or to him.

A pity, though, because we only manage to put ourselves into the same place. *Exactly* the same place. We draw a level for him and for us. It will have to be a low level, but there is no time to think about that.

And so we accept a level to which, in calmer moments, we should never dream of descending; we meet force with force—probably with still greater force.

Perhaps we may even go so far as to take pride in the fact that we are—and intend to be—the sort of person who will always speak out: a man may tackle us *once*, we say, but he will think twice before doing so a second time. That is where anger is so rough an abrasive; for, if we think twice before tackling *him*, we may keep his thoughts in place and our own at the same time; moreover, if it is to be a question of 'evenness' the philosophy still holds good because disturbing one's mind to such an extent leaves one weaker for the experience, not stronger. In fact, the difference between meeting anger with anger, and meeting it with tolerance, *lies in the evenness*. Instead of settling the affair (that is, if we really do settle it) on *his* level we may manage to settle it on our own; instead of sinking to his level we may raise him to what we like to think is our own quite *high* level.

That is where the importance of thinking comes in. No-one can expect to go through life without mishaps of this nature; sᶜmeone is bound to upset us sooner or later; but whoever is in the habit of thinking powerfully, and thinking the right thoughts, is always in a position to deal with such situations. It is the practised mind which applies a brake to the impulses. It is the quick, healthy brain which holds the emotions in full check and deals with the other man's mind in such a way as to hold *his* emotions in check, and thus to settle the affair on as high a level as is possible in the circumstances.

That anger and resentment are abrasives can be proved another way. Any philosopher will agree that one of the worst aspects of the wrong attitude of mind is the torture it can inflict *when one is alone*. Anger and resentment can then act on the mind with the roughness of a rasp.

Deep and painful mental abrasions are never more quickly —nor more surely—caused than by what I shall call 'negative rehearsal'.

Any of us may receive a letter which rouses our indignation to such an extent that we instantly begin rehearsing what we shall send in the way of reply. We may go so far as to spend some considerable time thinking it all out, adding to our vehemence by rehearsing our 'lines' until we consider they really meet the case. Even if we do not go so far as to write a word of what we have taken so much trouble to rehearse, *we are the worse for the rehearsal*. We have allowed a chain of thoughts, directed against someone else, to escape us. And, as I hope to prove beyond doubt later in this book, thoughts are too powerful to let escape in that way.

That reminds me of a very dear friend of mine (now dead some years) who is worth describing—at least, in light detail. He was a priest and had the heart of a priest. He was wont to say that not only did he refuse to suffer fools gladly, but refused to suffer them at all. When he said that his face lighted up with a smile that belied his statement; he was, as a matter of fact, a man with a heart of gold.

One day he showed me a letter from a woman in his parish. When I had read it I said: 'Do you often get letters like this? No-one has the right, surely, to attack a priest in that fashion? What are you going to do about it?'

'This is my reply', he said, handing me a letter he had just finished writing.

The reply was a masterpiece of satire and sarcasm. I do not think I ever read its equal.

'Well', I said as I handed it back, 'the lady will think twice before she writes to you again, I imagine. I wonder how she will take it?'

'She won't get it', he said. '*This* is what she will get.'

He then handed me a second epistle. This was clever in the extreme. Not a word out of place, not a word of complaint—much less of resentment – against her thinly-veiled insults. Such a letter could have only had one result: an abject apology. It was, as a matter of fact, a month before he received it; but he had it in the end. When I commented on the difference between his first and second reply, his eyes twinkled merrily.

'I wrote the first to prevent myself from going round to her house and boxing her ears', he said with a laugh. 'When I feel like that about some of these women in my parish, I get all the venom out of my system *before* I tackle them. I find I am the better for it.'

I forget what I said at the time, but I now think my dear friend was wrong. Perhaps it really suited him to get the venom out of his system, but philosophy would teach him —and others like him—that it is one thing to get poison *out* of one's mind, but it is a better thing to prevent it ever getting *in* there. Actually my friend was the worse for his preliminary rehearsal, but I could hardly have told him so.

To indulge in private rehearsal of a negative kind means that one *always* comes by the worse of it. The mental torture that can accrue from rehearsing angry scenes in advance has no limit; it can become so acute as to warp even a sweet nature; it can cause almost ceaseless misery. The power to think is the soul of man; no man's soul was given him to torture himself with.

Private rehearsal of a *positive* kind is another matter. Taking the vicar's incident again as an example, he could have written a preliminary letter as before; he could then have compiled a second letter as an improvement upon the first. Moreover, practice in the art of writing such letters would soon mean that no second attempt would be necessary.

To give him his due, knowing his real nature, is to say that he would go a long way out of his course to avoid hurting anyone; where his philosophy failed him was where he allowed *his own thoughts* to hurt himself. And yet he was so honest, and so humble in mind, that he could tell the story against himself by showing me the letters.

The thought brings us to the beginnings of a lovely, yet extremely simple philosophy. We all have the power to smile. We all know that a smile is a powerful vehicle for effect because we have seen smiles in others that have warmed our hearts. We all know that a man or woman who has a smile that might tame a tiger has something worth having. And philosophy would have us realize that we can do worse than use a smile as a beginning to our mental exercises, that we can let it contribute towards the job of levelling up our attitude towards others.

What is true of eyes that smile is true of voices. In their way they, too, can smile. It is indeed something to have gained such power of inflection as to make even a rebuke sound gentle. None of us need forget that the expressions of eyes, mouths, voices, are what people watch for most— *and remark upon most.*

It is largely a question of good thinking, which can well begin at home among those nearest us. Often enough, home may actually be the place where it is most difficult to begin; but home is where we do most of our philosophical thinking. Also it is likely to be where we exercise influence, where we experience most of our joys, even if most of our sorrows. However that may actually be in particular instances, if one is master or mistress in the home one can also be servant at the same time. That means, philosophically, that one's life there radiates light and warmth which, again, means that one has gripped the value of splendid thinking.

To get one's attitude towards others into a thoroughly good and workable condition takes more than a little thinking; but the answer is always the same: the power to think is the soul given to man by Almighty God at his quickening. It was given him to use.

Apart from the fact that there is always so much to think about which fascinates in the thinking, the power to think is all that survives any of us. It will last all eternity. So that laying emphasis on the importance of thinking is by no means waste of time.

Far from it, because thinking is a study in itself. The power to think *needs exercise*, and one of the best types of exercise for it is to devote time occasionally to thinking *about* thinking. If we are *really* thinking, we are bound to be conscious of a pleasant sensation of power. And a grand sensation it is!

Thinking, as an act, is capable of considerable subdivision. There is *subjective* thinking—important because it is about one's self, not necessarily *of* one's self. Very often it is an intimate form of thinking.

There is also *objective* thinking. Its importance is hardly assessable because it includes powerful thinking about others as well as thinking *technically*—which is always important.

There are, again, the impressions we take in—everything we absorb from nature, art, science, music, literature—and the sayings of others. Equally important are the expressions we give out. They are—or should be—the direct result of what we have taken in.

Finally, there is *projective* thinking, the most powerful kind of thinking we are capable of. These are all dealt with in this book. In my opinion they are all worth writing about because, added up, they put the capital L into Life.

No; it is impossible to lay too much stress on the importance of thinking.

II

SUBJECTIVE THINKING

As an expression, *subjective thinking* can easily be understood by rega ding it as something very intimate, something which proceeds from one's own consciousness, something closely connected with one's own personality. As personality matters very much—if any of us is to make a success of life here and do something worth while with it --the next step in the study of thought-production must be an examination of the thought-tendencies nearest ourselves.

A good beginning to a short study of subjective thinking may well be to contemplate our average condition of mind when we are alone for any length of time. As a plain question: *who of us is in any degree afraid to be alone?*

The answer to that question largely depends upon what we do with our thoughts when alone, especially when we are without anything particularly absorbing to think about.

There are many degrees of fear and many types of it; but fear, in the general sense of the term, amounts to a mental disturbance arising from expectation of evil to come, whether that expectation has a reasonable basis or not. Such fear sometimes arises from ignorance of quite elementary facts; at other times it comes from inability to appreciate the laws of cause and effect—but, whatever its cause may be, the sensation of fear is always unpleasant. It has a distinctly lowering effect upon the mind and consequently upon the body. If one's heartbeats are being accelerated by reason of fear, one can hardly expect to be in good form. Long before the sensation of fear increases to one of terror, anyone can be greatly discomfited. Lesser forms of fear, better known as nervousness, are bad enough; real fear is a tragedy.

If a person is fearful to any degree—whether of being alone, of being in the dark, of thunderstorms, of meeting strangers, of doing anything in public—there is something wrong with his thinking. As the only real antidote to fear is faith, the whole conception of fear turns back to something very vital but also something very elementary: does that person, or does he not, believe in a Supreme Power?

If a man does not believe there is a God at all he must have done a good deal of thinking of a negative kind—indeed, he must have gone to some trouble to come to such a conclusion. If he considers himself an agnostic, saying he cannot make up his mind, that he really does not know what to think, we at least can assure him we understand his position even if we do not agree with his views; but if he goes so far as to say, firmly and fixedly, *there is no God*, I (for one) must say—equally firmly and fixedly—that I do *not* believe him. I appreciate the fact that he is saying something he *likes* saying (for his own reasons, of course) but I shall feel inclined to tell him he is saying something he does not really believe.

For a good reason. *It is a literal fact that no system of positive atheism exists in the world.*

Even Buchner, the nineteenth-century philosopher, could not entirely deny the existence of God. He certainly did his best, but he was forced at last to conclude that 'God is nature'. He made the mistake most other negative thinkers of the world have made: he thought the soul of man was his brain and therefore perishable. Haeckel and Holbach thought the same. Holbach spent (perhaps wasted) years in forming a theory that 'matter and movement alone exist'.

And yet, for all these negative thinkers have thought and written, no system of positive atheism exists, or ever has existed. The only reasonable deduction it is possible to make from that is: *every intelligent human being, if held down to it, must confess there is a Supreme Power.*

Those who belong to any part of the Christian Church must have accepted a personal God and need no words to describe Him. The Testaments have furnished ample description. Anyone who is ready to declare that he believes in God recognizes in Him the Creator, almighty and omnipotent, and should (because of that recognition) already know at least part of the answer to the question about fear. He must surely have thought, at some time or other, that God is a power and can be (so to speak) *pulled at*. If you, personally, have never actually thought that, I hope you will begin thinking it now. I shall be quite content —at least, in this chapter —if you will allow that thought to remain with you; but, later, I shall want to develop that way of thinki. g much further.

Briefly, for the moment, God is here whether any of us trouble to think about Him, or not. He is here whether we are careful to use the transmitter He gave us at our quickening, or not. By the very laws of nature - He made those laws - we have the privilege of 'pulling' at His power; the more effectively we pull, the more power comes our way *by His answer*. Philosophy lays down that we are all here with a life to live, with an influence to exert, with a work to do. We can never escape that fact, merely because *we are conscious of our own being*. There we differ from the animals who are not conscious of their own being. Our dog may answer to his name but only to the sound of it — not because he *knows* it is his name, nor because he is conscious of his own soul.

We are conscious of our own souls because, unlike our pets, we have souls to be conscious of. And if we are conscious of our own being, can we imagine for a moment that our Creator has overlooked the fact that we are here? The more conscious we are of His existence, the more conscious He becomes of our own *because we are setting in motion forces of His own making*.

By those same laws any of us is at perfect liberty to 'throb the ether' just when we will. So that our first antidote to fear of the grosser kind is faith and the knowledge that we are here until we are sent for. We shall certainly not go one second before our time is up. Because of that knowledge the fear of sudden death need never greatly concern us even though, admittedly, such death is possible. We can well afford to dismiss the idea, if ever we have entertained it; or, if we like it better, we can brush it aside with the thought that sudden death is a quick way of going out. We shall get all the protection we ask for; and if we are

wise enough to realize that our existence on earth (as one
of His creatures) is not overlooked by the Almighty Creator
we can be comfortable enough on the other score.

Every second we spend in consciousness of the Supreme
is a second well spent. Neither need we spend more than a
second at a time, simply because God obeys His own laws.
He is good enough to think of (and for) us when we forget
to think of Him. That is obvious. All the same, the fact is:
we have our *own* power to attract *His* power. If we use that
power, fear is immediately beaten to death by knowledge
of power. The greater the power we obtain - perhaps the
greater the personal aspect of the faith to get that power—
the greater the antidote to fear.

There is another point about subjective thinking. It
concerns ourselves and our personalities before it concerns
anything. It therefore follows that the sum-total of our
subjective thinking makes up our personalities. Nothing
is more likely to weaken one's personality than a disposition
to worry over small matters. When we do that we make
ourselves less important in the scheme-of-things than we
need. When we do that we spoil everything for ourselves
and for others round us.

One of the prime causes of worry is ignorance of facts.
Anxiety, which is a form of fear, arises from the same cause;
but either can come about merely through deep affection
for others. It is so easy to be over-anxious for someone we
love; it can be extremely difficult not to worry (sometimes
quite unreasonably) about that person. Often enough it has
become obvious to us that, had we not thrown our reasoning to the winds, we might have saved ourselves much
disturbance of mind. Even when anxiety is the sole cause
of such disturbance, all that any philosopher can say in
reply is: 'Have you no transmitter? Why are you not thinking? You know where the only true power is.'

A hard answer? Perhaps it is, bare and unqualified; but
the fact remains that all of us are at liberty to absorb power
from the Source of it.

Even that statement is not enough; the matter cannot be
left like that. Neither will it be, but before it is possible to

develop even such a simple philosophy as this it must be made plain that our approach shall be humble. Otherwise there is little chance of success. I have something to say about meekness and humility later; but it is necessary here to say something about the attitude of mind which is the result of, and springs from, what is called the *inferiority complex*.

That complex is one of the worst mental maladies you or I can ever suffer from. How common it is! We both know people who are noticeably guilty of 'throwing their weight about', and we know that the cause for it is nearly always the same: lack of real knowledge coupled to a determination to hide deficiencies at all costs. Definitely 'at all costs', for the cost to the personality is often very high.

Conceit is another variation of the same low complex. Conceit is a fault that can affect us at almost any age, but it is perhaps most excusable in the young. A little learning is a dangerous thing at any time; one of its chief dangers is that it can cause anyone to imagine he knows more than he really does know, and to make him put on airs and graces that nauseate even those who love him best. The worst of it is: people whose own technique is sound are rarely slow to detect lack of it in others. Conceit is ever an *obvious* failing.

The inferiority complex is responsible for more than mere conceit: it is the prime cause of the worst possible attitude of mind—*jealousy*. That, also, is usually obvious.

Jealousy comes from an ungenerous outlook on life. No really generous person can be jealous. That jealousy can be extremely painful and difficult to deal with is too well known to merit discussion; it can be set down as the sign of a badly-balanced mind. No-one whose mind is well-balanced suffers from the agony of jealousy. He may be jealous *for* (on behalf of) someone; but that is not the same thing.

Generosity of outlook is what everyone needs if this world is to go round smoothly; especially do we need it if our critical faculties happen to be bright and brilliant.

When they are like that we see the faults in others in a
flash; we see their mistakes and we see why they make them,
but if we are generous in our outlook, if we are broad-
minded, gentle, understanding, our critical faculties are not
likely to let us down. We shall judge neither harshly nor
unfairly.   1.

The power to criticize is a grand power te possess —but
only when the possessor of it is generous. ʌ further point
about generosity is: *others quickly recognize it*. In consequence, even the most unlikely people respond to it. A
man who is really generous in his judgements of others
stands to lose nothing; he is always regarded as someone
to be relied upon. A man whose mind is warped with
jealous thoughts, and gives the game away by making
statements that prove what his mind is like, simply stands
to lose everything. His advice and counsel are rarely
sought—and that is another way of saying that he is valued
at his true worth. He is usually rated pretty low.

It is the generous mind which causes its owner to say
right things at right moments; the jealous mind is responsible for disparaging statements. It is all part of the
inferiority complex.

It takes a really generous-minded person to keep a perfect
balance when confronted with criticism from someone
whose own knowledge is either nil or markedly inferior.
Even when justified by facts, flat contradiction is rarely a
satisfactory means of dealing with such a situation—merely
because the type of person who will attack one in a violently
critical fashion is usually in no mood to accept contradiction, no matter how reasonable it may be. Often enough
the best card to play is a little well-directed humour. A
smile can be very disarming whereas a frown may only cause
the other man to buckle his own armour more tightly.

A grand thing to possess, humour! The best kind of
humour is part of the grace of God. So many people make
the mistake of never crediting the Almighty with a sense
of humour.

Such is a very short study of subjective thinking, of
thinking about one's self, and all round one's self. It has

to be well indulged in before any of us is able to make a success of objective thinking—much less of the more powerful *projective* thinking.

To make a success of the last-named we have to begin by being thoroughly conscious of the fact that we were sent into this world having been endowed with a power to think; until that was given us we were mere mass and matter. The fact that we came here at all was none of our own doing; but once we reached what is called 'the quickening', we were equipped with an immortal soul in order that we might take our rightful place in the ultimate scheme-of-things. That is saying that we are more important than we may have been disposed to imagine, for the God who accepted us as part of His purpose has *not* overlooked our presence here. That does make us important.

The point is interesting. We come here as the result of our parents' action. In that respect we do not differ from the animals. Moreover, the Creator had nothing to do with our personal advent even though He was originally responsible for the laws governing human life. Once His laws were made there was little if any interference on His part. Provided nothing went wrong in the pathological sense, the moment arrived when each of us *quickened* and—again, provided nothing went wrong subsequently—we each put in our appearance as an entity upon earth.

Some of us came unwanted; others of us came despite our mothers' efforts to prevent our coming; most of us were born in wedlock; some of us were less fortunate. But *all* of us went through the same physical process: we developed as mass and matter without sense or conscious-ness—or the hope of either—until that given second in time when the Creator honoured us (and our parents) by a flash on the ether. From that moment we were vitalized— we quickened; we became immortal. We became important in the great Scheme-of-Things. We were given the power to think.

Thus our power to think is the greatest power about us. The method by which we, as human entities, can absorb power from the only true Source of it forms the theme of

a later section in this book; but before that part of my
simple philosophy is reached the question of objective
thinking needs close attention, not alone for its own sake
but because it embraces our technique in everything we do.

III

OBJECTIVE THINKING

IT must be true to say that one's powers of concentration
are never quite what one would have them be. Few people
are likely to think otherwise. All the same, the power to
concentrate is so important—if one is to do anything really
well—that unless one's concentrative faculties work
satisfactorily it is quite possible to lose much in life which
might otherwise be gained.

We may recall our individual difficulties at school.
Unless we happened to be exceptionally studious our very
nature seemed to revolt against concentrating on anything—
unless it particularly interested us. On lovely summer
days, when we longed to be out in the sunshine, we were
compelled to remain indoors to learn pages of history or
French verbs; if not that, it was to wrestle with some
proposition of Euclid—*something*, anyhow.

To us, who resented the strain, there seemed nothing
right about it; but there was no way out, and so we stuffed
our fingers in our ears and did our poor best to commit
something to memory which persisted all the time in
slipping away. That we went the wrong way about the
job was probably not our fault; all that mattered was
whether or not we had spent the required time. We were
judged on results: either we knew our 'prep' or we did not
know it. The first state meant that nothing was said; the
second meant that a good deal was said, none of it to our
liking or personal comfort.

And yet, when the power to think was given us, the all-
wise Creator made the power to concentrate part of it.
In our earliest days we all exercised that power merely

because we had nothing else to do. Babies concentrate as part of their business in life. They are usually better at it than children of eight and onwards. That is because children of that age have learned to distinguish between work and play. To a baby play is work and work is play: it means full concentration either way.

Some years ago I chanced to be in a children's hospital. I visited the babies' ward. I did not actually count the babies in that ward, but I think there must have been at least twenty of them. What surprised me was: instead of howls, arising from such causes as discomfort or disapproval, there was complete silence.

'Do you drug your babies here?' I asked the Sister.

'We know a trick worth two of that', she answered. 'Go and see for yourself.'

I walked up to the nearest cot. Its occupant did not even deign to cast a glance in my direction. I offered what I considered to be a suitable salutation, but the baby maintained a dignified silence. He—it may have been she—was concentrating on the business of the moment. I then discovered that *all* the babies were concentrating. I doubt whether I have ever witnessed such perfect concentration before or since.

I soon found out the reason. Each baby had been given a tiny feather, and a dab of treacle had been applied to each of its forefingers. The feather stuck to the treacle. The baby, no doubt feeling the matter could not be left so unsatisfactorily, proceeded to pull at the feather which stuck to the *other* finger. Not fully appreciating the law of cause and effect, the baby took this seriously and set about working on what I privately thought was an unsolvable problem.

And so silence reigned. The babies were concentrating on their problems. Amusing as it was to watch, it occurred to me then that concentration is (or should be) an act of mental comfort, interest being the dominant factor.

In the days of our youth some of us experimented with a piece of white wood and a magnifying glass. We steered the glass about until the sun's rays began to burn the wood.

If we were sufficiently skilled we began on a pattern; perhaps we only burned our initials. Whichever way it was, we soon found out that causing the sun's rays to light up the wood was not nearly enough: we had to focus the glass until we actually produced *a picture of the sun* on the surface of the wood. As soon as the image of the sun appeared the wood began to burn; not before.

The act of concentration is like that. We steer the glass (our brains) about until it burns the subject in hand, which corresponds to the wood. Until our concentration is such that we have 'produced a picture of the sun' we are not driving our brains into our subject; but if we do produce the sun's image we are in splendid mental condition and can proceed to burn away merrily into our good works and pleasures.

For perfect concentration a great essential is personal comfort. A child who has been sent into a cold room for half an hour on a winter's morning to practise the piano is being badly treated. Who can practise the piano with cold hands? *Ask any concert pianist.* Who can be expected to concentrate on scales and exercises, or even a 'piece', before breakfast? *Ask the same pianist.*

At least reasonable comfort is indispensable to all work connected with the mind; but the power to concentrate is itself indispensable.

Concentration? A fickle faculty at the best. Unless we train our concentrative faculties they will lead us a fine dance. In order to train them it is imperative to set aside a few moments each day for the purpose. The best form of practice happens also to be the pleasantest: it is to let the mind rove about until it comes into line with some definite subject. Once that has happened the mind should be allowed to follow quite a leisurely line of review of everything connected with that subject. As a beginning to such a rehearsal (it *is* only rehearsal) the more familiar the subject the better; but the more the brain is coaxed in this simple manner the stronger will its action become. It is surprising how soon; and from the beginning of such practice the line-of-review can be shortened until the burning process begins within a few seconds. When that happens concentration has been achieved. It is a grand mental exercise.

Concentrating in this way *on something easy to retain* is the first step towards real memory-training. Most of us complain that our memories are not above letting us down. We are apt to declare that we remember faces but forget names, or else that we remember names but forget faces. We need not forget either if we go the right way about remembering both.

There is, if you require it, a splendid method of tying up the loose ends of an unreliable memory. Naturally, it begins with simple things. A good initial method is to spend a few moments last thing at night, just before sleep, in allowing the mind to rove a district well known to you. The better you know it the better will be the result, especially if it happens to be one which you can actually visit subsequently for purposes of correction.

Let your mind's eye take you along a road you know well— perhaps the one you live in. If the houses in it are named rather than numbered, you should recall the names of each as you mentally pass them. Who lives in each? You can pay an imaginary call—at least to houses where you have actually called at some time or other. Your 'visit' should allow you to produce mental pictures of any room you have been into; it should also allow you to meet every member of the household. You will recall their names and as much else about them as you can: what they wear, what their voices sound like; their expressions, their characteristic movements. By the time you have 'visited' half the road you may have dropped off to sleep, leaving your subconscious faculties to set the impressions. That does not matter; you can 'go' again the next night.

You can try to recall the names of people you have met or have been introduced to, together with at least a few particulars about them. People you have met on holiday, for instance. By deliberately waking up your memory in this simple fashion you will soon find yourself recalling both names and faces of people you have not even thought about for years. It is a simple thing to do, but it can have far-reaching effects if you elaborate the process, making your memory work a little harder each time you do it.

A powerful memory is invaluable; everybody knows it; but it cannot be called powerful unless it is retentive for small and great things alike.

It is largely a matter of interest. During the first great war I spent some time training boys in a preparatory school for their 'common entrance' examinations which they had to pass before they could proceed to their public schools.

Taking my usual form one morning, and finding that no-one in it had made the slightest attempt to learn the Latin conjugations I had previously set, I broke off from the lesson and asked for a little information. I pretended that I wanted it for some special purpose.

I asked for particulars of the scores made at the test match at Lord's the previous week. I was treated to a recital— not only of the scores I asked for but of what each batsman had made individually, of how each was out, as well as of details concerning the batting and bowling averages of the chief notorieties of both teams. I jotted all this down and proceeded to read it out. In doing this I deliberately made a mistake and was vociferously corrected.

Having completely hoodwinked the boys, I suavely commented on their 'great ability' to remember so many facts, but added that I was indeed surprised to find they had failed to remember *other* facts—namely, those connected with the present lesson. They seemed quite hurt, I remember.

The answer was that cricket interested them and Latin did not, despite the fact they all knew that failure to remember their Latin meant failure to pass common entrance at the end of term. And it all proved my contention that, if anyone desires to make his memory powerful he must first, of all train it in what interests him most. I should like to add a warning here: leave any form of mnemonics severely alone. There have been many so-called methods of memory-training, but most of them have proved to be nothing but a system of remembering one thing by another.

Thought-association *is* a power—a power to make the greatest use of; but if anyone wishes to remember something there is nothing like looking at it *and remembering what it looked like*. If you are not sure how a word is spelt, *do look it up* in a dictionary. A mere glance may not be sufficient; look at it again, and then reproduce it in your mind's eye. Look at it a third time—and *set* the impression. When you have made a habit of doing that you will never forget how to spell anything. A simple and direct method well worth bringing to perfection.

Developing this theme of simplicity reminds me to add that concentrating on *easy jobs*, until your technique is absolutely perfect, is another form of elementary memory-training. What actually happens is: you commit to memory the exact movements and also the order in which you make them. The easier the jobs the better start you are likely to make—a case of walking before you run.

For objective thinking a good memory is essential. For that matter, any advanced form of thinking pulls on the memory *and no mind will exert power unless it is well stored*. Apart from matters of technical interest and knowledge generally, a well-stored mind and a high-powered concentration are both worth attaining even if only because they can provide you with something to think about in circumstances which, by their nature, may prove extremely boring.

You may be compelled to wait on a platform for a train on a winter's night. Perhaps you have already inspected the waiting-room and have found one glance at it has been enough: a hall of gloom and no fire have suggested to you that your own society and the platform outside are preferable. It is on such occasions that your matured power to think out something can serve you really well; it is then that your power to spend time, rather than merely kill it, can be brought into play. So that when at last the waiting period is up, and you open a door and settle down in one of the nation's travelling dustbins, you may find that the unavoidable interval was not so bad as it might have been. At least you found solace in your own thinking and

are no worse for the experience. Having previously taken
pride in storing the cupboard of your mind, you managed
to extract enough from it to entertain you when you badly
needed entertainment.

So that the power to concentrate is the beginning and
the basis of objective thinking. The more one mind's sun
can burn its way into whatever is brought within its focus,
the more powerful does objective thought become.

After all, what we are in this world is the result of our
thinking. When we have succeeded in doing something
we particularly wanted to do, and have done it exceedingly
well, we are quite ready to believe our success *is* the result
of our good thinking. However frequently or infrequently
that may have happened up to the present, there is always
the future to consider - that is, if anything is to be made
of it. If we really desire to make our life one long crescendo
of sound, or if we only want to make ever so little noise
in the world, we have to call upon our power to think.
Fortunately, if treated well, it always responds; but unless
we live in our own minds what we really *want to be* we stand
a mighty poor chance of being anything very much.

The thought brings up the question of what is generally
called *ambition*: that is, the desire to be somebody or to do
something worth the doing. Ambition has often been
rated as a vice, but it need not be anything like a vice.
One can make a splendid virtue of it.

Aiming high is excellent; aiming ridiculously high shows
lack of judgement. There is reason in all things. Ambition,
rightly regarded and rightly used, is a splendid virtue.
It must be so because the Creator expects us to take ourselves seriously enough to desire to improve our outlook
on, and even our position in, life here on earth. There is
nothing against aiming at the moon in the hope of hitting
one of the stars so long as the moon is not plainly so far
out of reach as to make us ridiculous trying to reach it.

Man is *expected by his Creator* to believe in himself. If
that were not true it would also not be true that the world
has progressed by the efforts of outstanding men and

knows it. So that it comes to this: each of us is expected to trust himself to do anything within reason. You and I both need to ask advice of those capable of giving it; but we also need to remember that there is a Source-of-power ever ready to transmit vibratory power over us. We do well when we con bine the results we obtain from both sources.

In the doing of it all we have to mind our attitude—not only towards the Source-of-power Himself, but towards our fellow-creatures. It is the simplest philosophy imaginable that we shall be *eminently approachable*. If we are going to be what is neatly termed 'up-stage', we make a mistake of the first magnitude. If, after we have left this earth, an epitaph is required for a gravestone and our friends cause '*He was eminently approachable*' to be inscribed on it they will pay us a compliment that God Himself will appreciate on our behalf.

No-one is within his right to treat a fellow-creature as though he were an inferior. That, I think, is what Christ must have meant when he said: *judge not, that ye be not judged*. He could not have meant it in the legal sense because, in another passage, he spoke of a man being cast into prison after being *delivered* to a judge.

Perhaps it is our modern way of living that is the cause of our being class-conscious. If so, we cannot do much about it; but we can at least see that our consciousness of what we call 'class' is not misdirected. Class-consciousness there must always be in a society such as ours; but class-hatred is something to abhor. Nothing is truer, in this respect, than the proverb about birds of a feather flocking together.

So should they flock. Their 'pecking-interests' are the same. For this reason it can hardly be advisable for you to invite a bishop and a bookmaker to dinner on the same evening. Both may be fine birds, but the former might be facetiously described as a '*see*-bird'; the latter gets his worms from the turf. Their experience of spending an evening, even in your own charming company, may not prove successful.

You may have the deepest regard for your local police-

man, but you may hesitate before asking him to lunch for
fear he may not care about accepting. On the other hand,
he may be delighted to lunch with you. It largely depends
on who you are, not necessarily on who you *think* you are.

So that our various classes do keep us, as a nation,
divided and subdivided. There is nothing against such a
system—it seems to work well enough—but the moment
we suggest by our attitude that (in *our* opinion) anyone
else is our inferior, socially or intellectually, we exceed
our right. No-one who has done much objective thinking
can be a snob. In other words snobbishness is part of the
inferiority complex.

Important as these small considerations are, it must be
admitted that objective thinking is largely used for the sake
of gaining technique.

Poor technicians are but sorry creatures. It is not necessary
for you or for me to swell their ranks. There are too many
of them already. So that you and I are ever up against the
acquisition of greater and still greater technique, more and
still more scholarship and knowledge. Because of this,
neither of us can afford to cease thinking objectively. A
little learning *is* a very dangerous thing, but deep learning
is as safe as the Rock of Gibraltar.

The greatest reason for indulging in objective thinking
I have not yet given. I deal with it later, but I want to point
out, even at this early stage, that objective thinking and
concentration of the most virile kind on things worth while
mean that the mind grows more and more powerful every
hour of the day. Ultimately, objective thinking merges into
*pro*jective thinking—and that is a power well worth
acquiring. For the moment I can leave it, principally because
I want to say something about objective thinking in the
sense of a power over the body for its health's sake.

Much has been written on this theme. Many philosophers have asserted that perfect health can be attained,
and maintained, by perfect thinking. I am not disposed to
contradict the statement even though I think it needs a
good deal of qualifying. For one thing, I am quite sure that
it is easily possible to think mistakenly about health and to

do more harm than good. It always seems to me that the philosophers who insist that all disease can be cured by thinking the right thoughts—and only by that—are running a risk because there is such a likelihood of people doing the wrong things as a result of *immature* thinking.

Surely it is better to consult a physician, get his advice, and supplement that advice with good objective thinking. In the broad sense powerful thinking does a very great deal towards keeping any of us fit and well; but to suggest that one can keep fit and well solely by powerful thinking is more than I care to do.

Having been told what to do by a doctor who knows his job, what we do *with our minds* while the process of cure is going on is as important as the process itself. We do ourselves a poor service if we weaken our resistance by *thinking* weakly. The power over the body (which the mind *always* has in some degree) can be so increased by really powerful objective thinking that the whole body can be built up in such a way as to resist disease.

On the other hand, it is against the laws of nature if we detect a symptom and fail to set about a cure in the proper pathological manner. If we privately take the attitude we should take, it amounts to this: we have detected a symptom, probably as a result of pain; we consult our physician and obey him—but, *although we keep it a private affair*, we go to him as much as to say: 'Here is my trouble. You tell me what to do and I will do it. You can leave me to *make your cure effective*. I *know* how to think'. That is philosophical science. The more the power of the mind over the body is *rehearsed and exercised* the greater it becomes. There is nothing surprising in that, merely because it is a fact that everything connected with us follows some law of nature—and it is pretty feeble thinking if we forget that the mind swaying the body *is* one of the laws of nature. One of the most powerful laws at that.

The thought very naturally brings up the question of Christian Science. There is always a danger where Christian Science is concerned—at least, if its principles are carried to extremes. Christian it may be; but there is a doubt in my mind as to whether all of it is scientific, with all due respect to a number of people I have met who disagree with me.

Quite recently, a distant relative of mine became ill. She was an avowed Christian Scientist of many years' standing. She took the view that she was not really ill—or that, if she were, she would soon effect a cure without the help of any human agent.

Instead, she died. An examination proved that cancer was the cause of death, and a rider was added to the effect that quite a minor operation (had it been performed when the symptoms first became noticeable) would have been completely successful.

It is not my purpose here to say one word against Christian Science; but I would warn anyone interested in it to make reasonable, not unreasonable, use of it. I have nothing to say against the underlying principle of Christian Science; I could hardly do that because it would mean my modifying a firm conviction that the power of mind over the body is so great that almost *anything* can happen if that power is rightly used. Objective thinking can do much; it is the prelude to projective thinking which can do more. Projective thinking is a positive force. Sub-miracles are wrought by projective thinking.

By the way—a word about miracles. *Occurrences to be wondered at.* That is what they are; nothing more. At least, nothing more is suggested by the word's etymology.

The greatest of all miracle-workers was the Son of God. Not surprising, but the technique of some of his miracles was simpler than we may at first be disposed to think. Christ's power in this respect came directly from the Source-of-all-power. Translating the idea into terms of electricity, Christ was able to use *direct current*. He was connected with his Father by a line of ethereal rhythm. Thus the power he needed was always running into him, but it is interesting to note that the power he often used was little more than the power of mind over matter. Most of his miracles were simply thought out.

Again, not surprising; Jesus loved simple things. I only

mention his miracles here at all because, later on, I intend
to develop the main theme of this part of my book: that
the soul of man is his power to think and that there is a
Source-of-power whose strength may be absorbed by a
very natural means. You and I cannot expect to be allowed
to work by *direct current*, but there are such things as
'spiritual transformers'.

At all events, I propose to outline an experiment in time.
I trust you will think it worth making.

Before I get that far I do want to observe that it is
important—at this and all further stages of mental development —for you and for me constantly to revise our attitude
towards the Source-of-all-power. It is for us constantly
to assure ourselves that we are offering a complete acknowledgment of God as the Almighty Creator, an equally
complete trust that when we have mastered the art of
projecting thoughts towards Him *they will reach* Him;
a complete belief in the power of our own receiving-sets;
an absolutely clear idea of what it is we really want.

Neither of us will need a medium, spiritualistic or
otherwise. We need no intercessor. This is a private affair
and is best kept private. We each possess a personality.
The consciousness of who we are, and why we were sent
here, should never be allowed to escape us. It is for us to
see that such consciousness is firmly united to the greater
consciousness of the Creator whom we acknowledge as
eternal.

Eternal? An interesting word. What exactly does
eternal mean?

An obvious answer is *never-ending*; but obvious answers
are not always as accurate as they sometimes seem to be.
Here is a case in point.

Because Almighty God can never end He may be said
to be eternal. That is an accurate statement, despite
what Mr. H. G. Wells seemed to think when he wrote
God the Invisible King. To us, while on earth, God may
indeed be the Invisible King; but He is not finite. There is
nothing finite about Him. Neither is there about you or
me. We are not finite, except in the sense that our earthly

bodies are finite. There is nothing else about us that is finite. So that we and our good Creator are alike in at least one respect: He—and we—are eternal.

But there is something deeper about that word *eternal*. The fact that we were struck, when we quickened, with that immortal soul proves we actually *began at a given second in time*. We definitely *began*—here, on earth.

He never began.

And that is the difference between us and our Creator. It is an unthinkable thought, actually; neither you nor I can ever hope to work it out. It is easy enough to say: 'God will never end because He is eternal'. Vaguely, perhaps, it is possible to think that out—or, at least, to accept it as something sensible. Yes; just vaguely we can appreciate it; but when we say 'God never began' we hesitate. Then we add: 'Oh, well, I suppose He must have begun some time or other . . . millions of years ago. . . .'

No; we cannot say that. God is omnipotent—that is, powerful *without qualification as to power*. To that awe-inspiring statement God 'never began' there is no *possible* qualification. If God actually began there must have been a time, even if not measured, *before He existed*. That, again, means that there was a time when nothing existed which now does exist, that there was a time-space before anything connected with Him happened. Then, in that case, there must have been a point when time itself began and, *at that point*, God Himself must have begun. But there cannot have been such a time because no Being who is *omnipotent* and *infinite*—especially the latter, can have begun and *so have started to develop*. It is inconceivable that an omnipotent Deity began to grow and mature. It does not make sense.

Infinity and eternity work both ways. We can, as I say, vaguely appreciate that eternity goes on for ever, but when we realize that eternity means not only *for* ever but *from* ever we know that the mighty Creator of the universe never began and never can end: 'as it was *before* the beginning, is now, and ever shall be' . . .

And so time matters, as I hope to show later on. We have

all been guilty of wasting time, but the wisest of us know that 'making up for lost time' is really only a phrase. Lost time can never actually be made up. Even in eternity, though one imagines time is so insignificant as to be lost in it, there will not be time for all we want *unless* we make use of every moment of it.

And yet, here on earth, there is always—there should always be—time for leisure and thought. Time for pleasure, too. We do not waste time when we watch a beautiful sunset, or when we spend an hour absorbing something worth absorbing. We need to feed our minds with impressions, and time spent in gaining impressions is time well spent . . . but that is actually the theme of my next chapter.

The sun be-reds the river,
Windswept;
Soon 'twill be gone forever,
Unwept;
Yet my heart to its watching Giver
Has leapt.

The Sunset Gong has sounded in the dim nave.

I stand before the Crucifix
And pause to pray,
Lest I, forgetful of the hour,
Meet not (refreshed) the dawn
That heralds day.

IV

THOUGHT-IMPRESSIONS

BECAUSE life here is an experience, what we call 'experience' matters most in life.

Most of us cherish our pleasantest experiences and often enjoy the further pleasure of recalling them. We naturally try to remember what we really want to remember; we are hardly to be blamed when we try to forget what we find hurts and distresses.

Our experience is largely made up of thought-impressions —in other words, of what we have been able to absorb from our surroundings and environment. What we have seen and heard (and what we have *thought about* what we have seen and heard) all pile up in the mind and memory, leaving us in possession of what we regard as 'our experience'. Knowing we can do very little until and unless we have had experience, the wisest of us keep sufficiently awake to notice everything that goes on round us. That is always well worth doing because the memory of what we were in life, all we said, all we did, and—still more important—all we *thought*, is actually what we carry away with us at the end of our stay here.

So important are thought-impressions that everyone does well who regards them as the only perfect brain-food. To encourage the mind to open itself out to impressions is to find it ever ready and willing to comply.

The first principle to grasp is covered by what is called 'common observation'. Often enough the title is a misnomer. What should be common is very *un*common. Half the people one meets see only half what they should see and hear *less* than half what they should hear.

In these days of radio transmission there is plenty to hear, particularly in the way of serious music. My observation, as a trained musician, has caused me to make the melancholy discovery that a very high percentage of listeners to music only hear the top line—the melody; they do not listen carefully enough to become conscious of changes of harmony, much less of the presence of contrapuntal themes that make good music so satisfying to the ear. Unfortunately, not everyone is musical; all the same, it is sad to find that so many listeners never even notice a change of key. They listen, but do not hear.

What applies to music applies to every form of art. For he want of opening their minds, thousands of otherwise intelligent folk miss the whole meaning of art. And yet observation is one of the powers about us humans that absolutely cries out for exercise.

Ability to observe accurately is one of the things about us

that develops readily; it is a wonder more of us do not acquire that ability. You personally may be very wide awake; but if you are doubtful about the matter you can soon find out for yourself. You can review a day's activity— whether it be of work or pleasure—and carefully note what has taken place in it. Just what have you noticed during the day?

In the way of effort, training your powers for concentrative observation costs you little; neither should you find the process in the least boring. The next novel you read— will you notice its style? Will you notice the method of punctuation used by the author? Will you remember both title and author's name, together with the title of other books written by him? Who publishes the book?

How many of us fail to notice and remember what is said to us during the day! Some of us are more likely to sit on the edge of a chair and fidget, longing for someone else to finish what they are saying so that we can get in our own point of view. A good listener learns more than some of his friends who listen to nothing more interesting than the sound of their own voices; he sees more than his friends who forget to look beyond what they see in their looking-glasses.

I think it was old Archbishop Temple who glanced across a meadow, while being driven in a car, and said to the friend who was driving him: 'I wish I had a camera with me. If I had, I should certainly photograph those *thirteen cows*. They are standing so prettily.'

The cows were counted: thirteen was correct. You will agree that no man whose reflexes were slow, or whose mind was in anything but a beautiful condition, could have seen thirteen cows at once. Seven, perhaps; but not thirteen.

It is not necessary, judging by the Archbishop, to stare at one's friends in order to notice everything about them: their movements, their clothes, their voices. In a flash, if one's mind is in first-class condition, it is possible to take in everything about them. No-one need really ask his friends how they are; in five cases out of six one can see for one's self.

Doctors can do that sort of thing. It is their business, of

D

course; even so, that will not do for an answer. The fact remains that if a man's mind is absorbent there will be precious little that will miss him. Moreover, such power to observe, if trained to a high standard, makes man valuable to those who employ him as well as to those whom he employs. Such powers turn him into a man of the world; such powers really do lead him into high places and increase his importance.

That is why we were sent here. This life is a prelude. We were not intended to go through it wearing blinkers. In any event, we are here to enjoy anything and everything our good Creator has provided for us; also what our fellow-creatures have provided for us: one as much as the other. It is the duty of every one of us to lay our minds open to thought-impressions.

A small but quite effective beginning is an observation of the weather. Naturally we notice if it is wet or fine, but can all of us read an English sky? Can we tell by a glance at the clouds, at the direction of the wind, together with an inquisitive tap of a barometer, what the weather is likely to be? Most farmers can do it, but such knowledge is not necessarily their prerogative. Fishermen also can do it. Obviously it means much to them to be able to do it.

Incidentally, what is your personal attitude towards general weather conditions? Are you afraid of being out in storms, or fog, or great heat, or even great cold? Are you afraid of catching influenza in January or February because there is so often an epidemic of it just then? If you are, do not be surprised if you go down with it. You are acting directly *against* your power to think if you allow fearful thoughts of that nature to assail you.

Do you dread the March winds because it is a saying in England that March is 'treacherous'? Nonsense; you can afford to laugh at a March wind. Lovely April follows it, anyway.

The sooner you become indifferent to any type of weather the sooner will you cease to be depressed or adversely affected by it. Must you always put on a hat if you go out in the sun? The sun in this country will not hurt you unless you are afraid of it. Then it probably will, and all because you have lowered your resistance to it by means of a lowering form of thought. If there is a pathological reason why you should not expose yourself to it, that is a different matter, naturally; even so, you can always drive your brain against any *fear* of it.

As for thunderstorms, it really is a pity to be afraid of them. The chances that you will be struck by lightning are a million to one. You can afford to remember that the Creator has control of the lightning. English law has been founded on that fact, for if a man is killed by lightning he dies 'by the act of God'. You are not likely to die that way —at least, you can (as we say) 'take a chance on it'.

Electric storms are so gloriously vivid that watching them from a point of vantage is an experience well worth repeating when chance offers. They are so majestic. We can all afford to be babies over them and regard the noise of the thunder as the Creator's voice. 'It is the glorious God that maketh the thunder', wrote the Psalmist. Such words have an elementary thrill about them.

Do you remember that perfectly gorgeous storm during the late evening of St. Swithin's Day in 1945? The worthy saint must have thoroughly enjoyed it, for there was enough noise that night—when four storms were going on at the same time—to have reached the furthest limits of the universe, one would think. Fifty flashes of lightning every minute for nearly four hours—that is to say, only ten seconds in each minute without lightning. There were ramified flashes that lit up the country-side. Very few of them ever reached the earth; thus the damage was slight. It was just a grand noise—the sort of noise that made one take heart and realize that the King-Creator was Himself watching the operation of some of the laws He made and was good enough to give His earthly creatures an opportunity of enjoying it too. My only complaint was that there were no examples of ball-lightning which appears as a luminous ball in the heavens, only disintegrating and breaking up explosively on contact with some object in the air; but there were thousands of forked flashes.

A magnificent display of Eternal Power. I know that the impressions I gained from watching it that night have remained with me ever since.

Have you ever seen Scafell Pike, the highest point in England? His home is in the lakes. It must be the best part of three-and-a-half thousand feet from the floor of Wastwater to his peak.

He knows what thunderstorms are. He is used to two hundred inches of rain in a year and thinks nothing of them. A land of rain. It can rain in the Styhead Pass as nowhere else in these islands. To be caught in a shower there may be to accuse the Old Man of Coniston of having rather a silly sense of humour; to spend a fortnight of completely fine weather in the Lake Country is something you can expect to happen once only in your life.

Yet, do you wonder that Wordsworth adored the Duddon Vale? Do you wonder that he spent sixty out of his eighty years in this, his native country? Or that Southey lived at Keswick for forty years? Or that Coleridge spent so much time with the Wordsworths at Grasmere? And what about Ruskin who lies buried at Coniston? And all the rest of them: Shelley, Scott, Carlyle, Keats, Tennyson, Matthew Arnold, and Mrs. Hemans? Does it not seem obvious that these literary-minded souls, who all lived by their pens, went there *because of what they could absorb in the way of thought-impressions?*

They deliberately went to that magic land, that land of transformation scenes where storms arise out of less than nothing, where rain lashes down the cragsides and God's lovely thunder shakes the Cumbrian mountains with glorious, deep music; where blue-and-gold lightning rips the sky like parchment; where winter snows melt in already ice-cold waters.

Why did they go there? *Merely to absorb inspiration from the wonders of nature.*

But surely you have seen something of the kind, if not actually there? Has not the experience fed the very cells of your brain? Has such an experience not sent your thoughts flying ahead of you, beyond --far beyond—Scafell Pike (or any other mountain you may have seen) and made you deeply conscious of the Maker-of-all-these-things?

Surely it must have been so. You must have absorbed something, and have come away the richer for having done it. Surely you must have been conscious of the Lord of Creation and He, in His unfailing courtesy to you as one of His earth-creatures, immediately became conscious of you. Compared with such grandeur, you may indeed have felt insignificant; but the Source-of-all-power does not regard you in that way. In His eyes you are more important than all the mountains in Europe.

There are quieter impressions than these. Have you never slept in your own garden? If you have, you must have absorbed many thought-impressions. You must have felt you were on holiday until the morning. You may have been quite unable to decide why the Plough was so named because you yourself would be sorry to plough anything at the perilous angle it assumes in the northern sky; but by the morning you had probably forgotten all about it, or else have concluded that it had fallen into the sea. But it was there again the next night.

Your waking impressions must have been adorable. How enchanted was your garden! The shadows seemed to be slanting all the wrong way in the early eastern sunlight. Everything looked different. But that was because you had slept. A new day had come. And even if a dream had come your way it could only have been an English midsummer night's dream. And so you rose from your soft, sweet sleep —the gift of Him who never sleeps.

Surely such impressions affected you? Your mind must have been revitalized. You had absorbed the loveliness of an English summer night. The experience fed your brain-cells, and you were prepared for another day of work or pleasure. It hardly matters now which it was. In the long run, at the end-of-things-here, it cannot possibly matter how many days you devoted to pleasure, what happiness and enjoyment you found. All that can ever matter is that your life had a meaning to it, that you drove your brain ahead, that you used your power to think, that you worked well and faithfully, helped others, shed radiance round you.

You can always open your mind to impressions of nature and be the better for having done so. You can watch the setting of the evening star and let your mind rove beyond it awhile; you can let the consciousness of its presence make you conscious of the God who made it and set it in the heavens —and you need not wonder what good *that* has done you!

These observations are not intended to be digressions from my main theme. I think too much of the importance of thought-impressions to allow them to be that. If they disturb your memory of equally vivid impressions at this moment my purpose will have been served.

I remember standing at Land's End, looking out westward across the deep Atlantic towards Newfoundland, three thousand miles away. Nothing but sea. I remember it occurred to me that, were it not for a certain strange phenomenon which works according to the laws of the God of nature, I might have been standing in perishing cold instead of in the warmth of one of old Father Neptune's sweetest sea breezes. I know I began wondering whether the old chap ever lived, but decided to relegate him to the mists of Greek mythology—where he belongs. Still, allowing him his existence for the moment, Neptune is a grand fellow. I remember thinking that the sea has made us what we are as a nation—or, at least, that my father used to tell me so when I was little.

I have watched Father Neptune playing at changing from purple to green and back again, or from a deep blue to a dull grey; I have laughed at him when he has taken it into his old head to try to wash away the promenade I was walking on, and I have paid him due homage in my admiration of his efforts when (I felt sure for my personal entertainment) he has hurled his spume a hundred yards inland; and I have thanked him for one of his special parades of nice white horses that galloped for my pleasure along the horizon. I suppose the old fellow knows his own value. He knows quite well we cannot do without him. Still, he is good to England.

I remember gazing across his expanse at Land's End before regretfully turning away towards towards *England*; and I listened to the sea-birds screaming as they gave exhibition flights from the Longship Lighthouse to the mainland. One and all, they screamed *'Land's End, Land's End!'* To me, at that moment, it seemed to be the world's end; but I made my way eastward knowing that all England lay before me. I knew I should soon pass the first farm in it (it was the *last* farm as I came out), the first brook, the first hedge, the first tree. I had the manners to remember my grace. I said : 'Thank God for the Gulf Stream!'[1] . . .

* * * * *

If you look inside a piano you will see much machinery. If you peep through the f-holes of a fiddle you will see no machinery. Because it is a machine the piano does not improve with age; a violin does.

The mind of man is like both the piano and the violin. It is like the piano because, being a machine, it must be used to remain in perfect condition. It is like the violin because it improves with age.

For this very reason, the all-too-prevalent notion that a man is 'too old at forty' is wrong. Such a statement will not stand up to a moment's examination. A man may be too old at forty to play rugby football or water-polo; but for mental life and vivid outlook he is not too old at *twice* forty. Yet how often it has been said — and, unfortunately, believed — that to appoint a man or woman to take on a piece of work after the age of forty is an unwise proceeding. People who believe that forget that if a man is an artist, a writer, a composer, a doctor, he is not thought to be anything like too old at forty. As for bishops and prime ministers, not many are appointed until they are well past that age. The theory—if such it can be called — has been badly thought out. Experience is what tells in the long run.

[1] These impressions were recorded in a slightly varied form in *English England* (Muller, 1931).

The gaining of experience is a natural process. Just *being here* for, say, half-a-century accounts for most of it—just being here and noticing what goes on all the time. Doing the same things until one can do them perfectly and seeing to it that nothing is done to slow down the process. Gaining experience can be amazingly slow unless something is done to speed it up. Being satisfied with such experience as one can hardly avoid accumulating is rather like letting an engine run without taking on a load.

There is so much here to help us. If we are attracted by music and yet have no opportunity to become a performer, we can at least regard music in its proper light - as an influence and a power. The laws of harmony and counterpoint were thought out by men of genius. Moreover, in these days, one can come to know the greatest music merely because so much is performed and broadcast in the course of a twelvemonth.

Music is a divine art. It is a power in this world of ours; in the next world it must be something very much greater: it must be a living, vibrant force. No doubt much of it is written and performed by musicians who distinguished themselves on earth: I know I have often thought that John Sebastian Bach must be the organist-in-chief in the Temple of the Eternal. If I find I am mistaken, I shall indeed be surprised.

Perhaps all the arts are divine? I should be the last to advocate that everyone study some form of art—merely because gifts and tendencies are so diverse; also because we need scientists and mathematicians. On the other hand, I do say emphatically that intelligent love for one of the arts brings with it a great spiritual power.

After all, we have to remember that the arts are *here*; they surround us. We can never hope to adjust our minds finely if we allow nothing artistic to enter them. We are missing things if we ramble through life without absorbing beauty from what we find so near at hand. If you, personally, are attracted by architecture you can hardly pass a beautiful building without experiencing a sort of thrill. In some lovely church or cathedral your mind can be fed handsomely;

perspective will play tricks with your vision until lines you know to be parallel assume, in the distance, angles that surprise you.

Yet half the people who walk up Ludgate Hill hardly notice St Paul's. It might not be there. But the possessor of a mind receptive to beauty is entertained by every line of its western towers. In a very real sense Sir Christopher Wren was an earthly god who saw, in the lines of perspective, the Mind of the God he revered so humbly. Only a humble man could have conceived St Paul's.

That kind of humility springs from deep knowledge and scholarship; it is part of the superiority complex. How often has one read that Christ was humble! Yet you or I might have mistaken his humility for something very different had we been present and heard what he said about the Scribes and Pharisees. Had we been together in the Temple the day he flogged the moneychangers and drove them into the street, we might have found it hard to reconcile such an exhibition of righteous anger with the humility he was known to possess. Yet the Son of God was humble · very humble whenever he spoke his Father's name; on the other hand, again, he was proud to be the Son of an eternal God. He was strong in his humility. So it has been with many great men since.

It certainly was so with the man who built over eighty churches and a great cathedral in London. He was England's greatest architect; he was too great ever to forget, for one moment of time, that there was only one real Architect— and if any man ever enjoyed absorbing impressions that man was Christopher Wren.

He began his scholarly life as a scientist and an astronomer; he held a professorship in the University of Oxford. It was not until he went abroad, and absorbed every line of the greatest buildings he saw on the continent, that he even thought of being an architect. What had happened was: he had filled his mind with lovely thought-impressions. He then came back to England burning with a desire to turn those thought-impressions into thought-expressions. And, at the end, when his work was done, he took to contemplation and reading good literature, the Bible most of all.

If, as the result of anything I have written here, you yourself think it worth while to spend time absorbing thought-impressions, I beg you to take every chance of hearing good English spoken--not alone for the subject-matter, but for the sound of wonderful words.

Did you chance to hear the broadcast of *Murder in the Cathedral?* Perhaps you saw the play itself? Do you remember these lovely lines? May I suggest you read them aloud to yourself now, listening to the beauty of their sounds:

> I have lain on the floor of the sea and breathed with the breathing of sea-anemone, swallowed with the ingurgitation of the sponge. I have lain in the soil and criticized the worm; in the air have flown with the kite. I have plunged with the kite and cowered with the wren.

Or this, from Dryden's *All for Love*:

> Pleasure forsook my earliest infancy; the luxury of others robbed my cradle and ravished the promise of a man . . . Had Cleopatra followed my advice, then had he been betrayed who now forsakes. She dies for love, but she has known its joys. Gods! Is it just that I, who know no joys, must die because she loves?

There is a passage in Marlowe's *Edward II* which may ring a little in your ears:

> You villains that have slain my Gaveston!
> And in this place of honour and of trust,
> Spencer, sweet Spencer, I adopt thee here:
> And merely of our love do we create thee
> Earl of Gloucester and Lord Chamberlain,
> Despite of times, despite of enemies.

These, especially the first and last, are such *English* English; true, timeless English; English expression of English thoughts.

Yet the English language is unparalleled as a medium for the expression of sentiments not in the least English. Did you see Flecker's *Hassan?* If you did see it, you must hardly have forgotten the exquisite pain you suffered when you heard Malcolm Keen, as the Caliph of Baghdad, thus addressing poor Safi:

> If I impale thee for conspiracy, how shall I burn thee for blasphemy? If I skin thee for thy impudence, how can I flog thee for thy folly?

There is more of this unpleasantry, but the Caliph is interrupted by Safi himself who, having lost patience, demands to know what must be his condemnation.

And the answer, inexorable, cruel, yet superbly dignified:

> For lunacy to be nailed, for conspiracy to be stretched, for blasphemy to be . . . *split!*

English alone could represent such appalling, lovely horrors. And yet, when Hassan declared his love for the sweet Yasmin, surely there could never be anything more exquisite than the voice of Henry Ainley as he chanted:

> Or when the wind beneath the moon is shining like
> a soul aswoon
> And harping planets talk love's tune with milky wings
> outstretched, Yasmin,
> Shower down thy love, O burning bright; for one
> night or the other night
> Will come the Gardener in white—and gathered
> flowers are dead, Yasmin!

What sounds! I beg you to read them once more—*aloud.* And do you remember the end of the play, when the divine music of Delius lifted these lines to heaven? :

> Sweet to ride forth at evening from the wells
> When shadows pass gigantic on the sand,
> And softly through the silence beat the bells
> Along the Golden Road to Samarkand.
>
> We travel not for trafficking alone;
> By hotter winds our fiery hearts are fanned;
> For lust of knowing what should not be known
> We take the Golden Road to Samarkand.

What a language ours is! And, even now, I have passed by a certain William Shakespeare—out of fear, chiefly; for where can I begin, and having begun, where end?

Yes; listen to great English. Much can you absorb from it, your own tongue. For him who can write it perfectly there should be a laurel-wreath, or else a halo.

And finally, at least, on this part of my theme, you and I can always add to the power we have gained from our day's impressions when we review all that has happened during that day.

It has been a day's experience. What have we gained from it?

A day is just a convenient division in time; out of every twenty-four hours we are likely to spend eight in bed. That need not disturb us so long as the other sixteen have not altogether been in vain. Surely we have gained *something* in the way of power? Surely we have added something to our store of experience? Yet, what we have stored away is not quite *safely* stored unless we review it before we sleep. We shall probably fall asleep while holding the actual review; but that does not matter. We can safely leave the rest to our subconscious faculties; *they are always glad to do a job for us.*

What really matters is: we have set the day's impressions. The mistakes have been reviewed, not allowed to go unnoticed. Likewise the day's successes. For us the day is past and over. It can never be lived again, save in the memory alone. But there is another day tomorrow, even though when 'tomorrow' comes we have to call it 'today.'

And so we live each day as a separate period of time in our lives; before we sleep we should look it over calmly and dispassionately, deriving such satisfaction as we may from the best we can find in it. We should take account of our dealings with others, our general bearing, our temper, our finer attitude, our most secret thoughts. We should then lie down to take our rest, having seen to it that while we held the review we were conscious of the Heavenly Reviewer. We should lay before Him one *day's experience of life.* That day, however we have spent it, is important because it has been a rehearsal for the day following it.

That is how life is made up here. If, on first awakening,

we regard the new day as something worth while living, by the time we lie down again that night we shall have found it has been worth while to have lived it, if only for a few grand moments in it. If we are courtly enough to flash our thanks to the Creator for anything in it we may have enjoyed, for anything that has given us the least satisfaction, *we make Him conscious of our contentment*. A God who is Love personified will hardly resent that. He is more likely to be content at our contentment.

All of which points so strongly to the importance of each day. After all, days do make up life here. For that matter, days will make up life hereafter because eternity itself is likely to be made up of days. Eternity may be a very long time, *but it is not a very long time made up just anyhow*.

So that the day's impressions are important. To open one's mind to them, never to cease being on the watch for them, is a simple philosophy worth carrying into effect. Whether our impressions assail our minds as though blown in on one of the four great winds of heaven, whether they are found in the dales and vales and wolds and wealds, whether they come with the trill of a bird or the bleat of a lamb, in deep winter or high summer, with the bursting buds or the last of the leaves, does not matter. If we have been thinking objectively as well as subjectively thinking for others as well as for ourselves, we have been absorbing part of the Mind of God—and something very like *majesty* enters our immortal souls.

And sometimes, when you personally are tired and in need of reviving strength for your good purposes, if you gaze at beautiful pictures you will often find peace of mind. Or if you go into some ancient and beautiful building especially if you are lucky enough to find it empty. You will indeed be unreceptive if you do not discover that, in such solitude, you are *least* alone.

Perhaps, at some other time, you may chance to be in a vast cathedral where—I really do hope this for you— there is an organist who can play the music of Bach. If ever you are so fortunate, I beg you to stand still and let

the throb of the deeper pedal-notes vibrate upon your
body. Make your mind a complete blank, and let the sounds
of a cathedral organ sweep over you. Let your mind dream
awhile. . . .

> Methought I heard the deep'ning roar
> Of multitudes of oceans
> That hurl'd the surging surf
> Against a thousand crags.
> It rose and fell as if
> The Judgement Day itself were nigh,
> And earth in twain were split.
>
> And then great colonnades of arches
> Seem'd to rise from out the sea.
> A carvèd roof,
> A noble nave with echoing aisles,
> A snow-white marble altar,
> A crucifix of amber.
>
> And in the flick'ring light of a lamp
> That burn'd before the shrine
> The organ was reflected.
>
> And there an agèd master sat,
> Bewigg'd, array'd in courtier's dress.
> On and on he played.
> And then I knew the sound of what
> I had thought to be the End-of-Things
> Was John Sebastian Bach
> A-thund'ring out the cadence of
> His *Great G Minor Fugue*.

V

THOUGHT-EXPRESSIONS

DELIBERATELY seeking for power for one's personality by absorbing thought-impressions has a deep and
lasting effect upon the mind *which refuses point-blank to go
on absorbing without giving out again*. If, on the other hand,

we make no effort to help it to give forth we do less for ourselves than we need, and certainly less for others.

By making a habit of absorbing we become collectors-of-impressions; we make a habit of learning; we tend towards scholarship. And the process, once begun, goes on and on. Once we have acquired the habit of absorbing we never give it up. It never leaves us, day nor night—*day* because the mind becomes more and more receptive as time passes, *night* because the subconscious mind takes over while the brain and body rest.

The result of this: we reach a kind of saturation-point when the mind refuses to take in more without first giving out. We are not allowed to keep our own secrets. If we learn little we cannot give out much—that is obvious; but the converse is just as true. What we absorb we are bound to expel in some form or other.

Most of us have met people whose minds are well stored and who have the lovely gift of being able to fascinate by their delightful way of conversing.

To possess a charming personality is to possess something worth having—not least because there is so much *reflected* pleasure in one's own mind. The other kind of personality also reflects in one's own mind, but the reflection is distorted. These are the extremes, and the result of either is too easily appreciated to need much comment. There is, however, a mean between the extremes which requires looking at. It is one's realization of a *growing* personality.

If a man's personality is actually growing (by reason of his own admirable efforts regarding it) he needs to avoid the inevitable growing pains. Such pains are not pleasant. If that man finds himself in the company of others, whose intellects have not reached out as far as his own, he may commit the mistake of slipping off his balance. Lack of experience may cause him to feel *what he mistakenly conceives to be his own superiority* is something he can show off to advantage. What he *thinks* is superior is actually inferior because he does in a sense try to 'show off'. All forms of 'striking an attitude' are part of the lower complex. Most of us have seen something of the kind in young people; if we are wise we shall put it all down to growing pains and hope for the best.

So many of us forget that if our conversation leaves other people feeling (although we know what we are talking about) that they themselves ought to be ashamed of their own ignorance, we are suffering from something we should watch. We are suffering from the pain our growing personality puts us through, and we are actually inflicting pain upon others *whose sensitiveness is disturbed by our attitude*. The matured personality brings to life something very different: we give our information but in such a way as to make others feel they knew more than they thought they did. If we can get so far as to make other people feel that way, they automatically rise to a higher level after listening to us. In that case we may consider ours to be the beginnings of a really beautiful personality; our growing pains have evidently subsided.

It is for you and for me to impart knowledge where it is required, but the superiority complex should rise within us while we do it. When it does, we cause others to feel *we respect their knowledge*; only the inferiority complex within us allows them to think *we despise their ignorance*. If we make someone else feel a fool we have done very little for him—certainly nothing he will ever thank us for. Far more likely is he to remember the fact; having been thus bitten, he will be shy the second time. We have crushed his spirit—and who is any one of us to do that?

The thought reminds me that I was (some years ago) sitting with that most charming of writers, E. V. Lucas, in his office at Methuen's in Essex Street. During conversation one of the other members of the firm said something—I cannot now recall what—about a certain person being 'a perfect gentleman'.

'E.V.', as we all called him, looked mischievous. He often did. Knowing his sharp wit, I thought it might be diverting to bait him. I fear I was often guilty of that where he was concerned, but it was worth while because I usually received a grand piece of satire for my pains.

'What *is* a gentleman, E.V.?' I asked, winking at the other man.

He, too, looked expectant. He knew, even better than I, what E.V. could do when skilfully baited. But E.V.'s eyes did not twinkle with mischief this time, nor did his mouth curve up in its customary whimsical fashion. Instead, he put his hands in his pockets and gazed out of the window down Temple Gardens.

'A gentleman?' he mused.

Then, after another pause, he said quietly: 'A gentleman is he in whose presence no-one can ever be made to feel uncomfortable.'

Well? Can you beat it? Can you give a better definition of a gentleman (and presumably a lady) than that? I confess I cannot get anywhere near it. It is the best definition of a gentleman I ever heard—but, then, E.V. could define anything when he was put to it.

The power to make everyone comfortable in one's presence is assuredly a power that is semi-divine. Perhaps wholly divine, for who can ever have felt uncomfortable in the presence of the Son of God? None of his friends, certainly; none, indeed, but they whose own consciences rebuked them. It was this very quality, which characterizes all true gentle men and gentle women, that Christ showed so unfailingly. In every sense was the Son of God a gentleman.

How personality matters! An attractive personality is irresistible. We all recognize the fact because we have all had our heroes and heroines. We shall never cease to have them. Whole continents can be swayed by a great personality.

There is another thought. Perhaps *we* are heroes or heroines for others? Have you yourself ever thought you might be someone's idol? Can you think—at this very moment—of someone who has made an idol of you? If you can—and I am pretty sure you can—you must have recognized that you are saddled with considerable responsibility. Being someone's idol is no light matter. He or she who worships at your shrine, who admires and loves

E

you for what you are, demands much from you. If you take proper pride in your personality you will never let that person down.

On the other hand, to make it one's aim and object to *be* an idol for everyone is a poor thing to do: heroes and heroines are never self-made; but it is true to say that being deeply respected often *creates* qualities only to be found in heroes and heroines.

If your personal evidence of power, your adorable serenity, your complete approachability, have been the reasons why you have become someone else's idol, your superiority complex—that power which deep thinking alone can give you—will drive out every vestige of the complex inferior. Because of that you automatically raise yourself to the level your hero-worshipper believes you are on. Once you realize you have attained such a position in the eyes of someone else it may take some thought to keep up such a position; but the power to attract *is in itself* so attractive that it is something you can never afford to lose.

It is only when we attract that we really prove our spiritual worth; it is only when we attract that we make plain how deep is the power within us. It is only when we attract that we give good reason for our being here at all. It is only *because* we attract that we are missed when we have to leave. With personality we can conquer our own little world of friends and acquaintances; bereft of it we are spiritual outcasts.

Personality is never more vital than when we essay to teach. The office of a teacher is a grand one. We deal with someone who has sought our counsel because we are reputed to have knowledge. That pupil comes to learn—not to be told he knows nothing. It is a question of making that pupil comfortable in our presence. The moment we show the least sign of scorn of his ignorance we set a barrier between him and us. We might just as well let him go home without his lesson for all the good we are likely to do him. If a pupil is to absorb thought-impressions from our own thought-expressions (and that is what he comes for) we must put everything in front of him in a way that absolutely thrills him. Otherwise, we fail.

It is the ability to thrill a pupil that makes of any of us a fine teacher.

The greatest teacher of all was Jesus himself. It hardly strains your imagination, or mine, to picture the rapt attention of the heterogeneous crowd of people sitting on the mountain-side. The deep musical voice of the Son of God, as he uttered the beatitudes, must have been heard in deep silence.

While I think of it · the term *beatitudes* reminded me—there is one of them I should like to comment on: *blessed are the meek, for they shall inherit the earth.*

Did Christ really say that? I wonder. Naturally, most people like to regard the Testament as being above suspicion. The fact is: in many places the mind of a Greekist is left in doubt. The English scholars employed by James the First to translate for our benefit were occasionally guilty of mistranslation. I think this is a case in point.

I admit that the word *praeis* in Greek does mean *meek*, but I also remember that Jesus was not speaking Greek at the time. He understood Greek. I do not doubt that he spoke it as fluently as any native of Athens because Joseph must have spoken it; but the fact remains that he was not speaking Greek *then*. He never made a habit of speaking Greek while teaching. Instead, he spoke Aramaic because his audiences spoke it. Probably not more than one per cent of that crowd on the mountain-side understood Greek to any extent.

The Aramaic Jesus spoke was not even the literary Aramaic of Jerusalem. When talking to a man like Nicodemus, who was himself something of a scholar, Christ would probably have spoken the finer kind of Aramaic; but when talking privately to his disciples or when addressing a country crowd he spoke the dialect known and understood by the peasants of Galilee.

So that it is quite possible that *praeis* was the best word in Greek which could represent what Christ actually said in Aramaic. Furthermore, when it came to translating the

Greek of the New Testament into English in the days of
James I (in 1611) *meek* may have been what the translators
considered the best rendering of *praeis* into English. Also,
one must remember, the English word *meek* may have had
a slightly varied meaning in Stuart days; it 'may not have
had the meaning it has in these.

The Oxford Dictionary suggests it means *humbly sub-
missive*, though it takes care to add a note to the effect that
meek people are those easily 'put upon'. *Blessed are the easily-
put-upon?* Hardly.

Strangely enough, the French translators have made a
better job of the passage than we have. Here it is in French:

Heureux sont les débonnaires, car ils heriteront de la terre.

Debonair? Grand. Excellent thought. I can accept it.
Debonair, in a sense, also means humble. I should say it
even means *graciously humble*. Indeed, I should be inclined
to go still further and suggest it means *pleasant-minded*.
That thought I like best of all. Blessed are the *pleasant-
minded*, for they shall inherit the earth, but the 'easily-put-
upon' are not likely to inherit anything much.

This little digression is not without point merely because
the *whole* point with regard to humility is: *there is always
strength about it*. Any really humble-minded person has
found out a good deal about life. For one thing, he has
found out how little he knows and how much there is for
him to learn. For another, he has taken pride in what he
really does know; but he has not made such a song and
dance about it that everyone else mistakes that pride for
vanity. In other words, he has the superiority complex
well developed; he has learned how to take his place among
his friends, to 'behave himself wisely'; and therefore 'to
do well'.

For real honesty of purpose humility is indispensable.
If one is really humble in mind one must also be honest in
mind—and the God of the world loves honesty. If one is a
braggart or jealously minded, one must be spiritually
dishonest—and the God of the world is compelled to
regard any such person with mixed feelings. If ours is the
complex superior, we must be conscious of life in its

highest and most exalted form. *If ours is the complex inferior we must have been wasting a colossal amount of time trying to make others believe we are better than we can ever hope to be.*

It is the humble soul becomes the finest teacher. Think, for a moment, of all the masters and mistresses you ever knew at your own school. I am thinking of those at mine. I can subdivide them for you with the greatest of ease because I subdivided them long before I left the school.

Out of a staff of twenty-five, at least five were hopeless. We ragged them all through the lessons they gave. In three cases it was really a pity we did so because they were such grand teachers; but there was always a buzz of conversation going on all over the classroom.

One of these, I remember, was the science-master. As we always had the fatuous practical jokers with us, someone was sure to turn on the jets of something unpleasant. There was nearly always an appalling stench of carbon bisulphide or sulphuretted hydrogen.

Had the Greek master been the science master, there would have been nothing of the kind. His personality was far too grim. There was no nonsense where he was concerned. When he was about we behaved ourselves—or took the consequences.

We learnt from all these men, but some personalities seemed to invite ragging. Then there was the French master whose attainments in the linguistic world (we knew he spoke nineteen languages fluently) were so dazzling in our eyes as to make of him something like a demigod. He had only to move a finger to obtain rapt silence. We hung on his every word; we strained our ears to appreciate his amazing pronunciation of French which, we knew, had time and again been quoted by French scholars as perfect. This man was actually a Greek by birth and had been educated in Constantinople, but we sat in breathless silence even to hear him read out the marks or give out a notice brought round by the porter, so perfectly exquisite was his utterance of every English word he used.

Apart from this, he was approachable. He never made

any of us feel uncomfortable. Someone would be sure to ask him a thoroughly inane question that made us all laugh; when that happened he would laugh with us—but the next second he would answer that question in such a way as to make the poor mutt, who had made such a fool of himself, laugh as much as we laughed. Even so, I remember, we all learned something from his answer to even the most stupid question.

To us he was a hero. He must have known it, but he never gave away the fact if he did know it. His humour was grand, his dignity superb.

Dignity? What a thought! *Personal dignity*. Is it worth writing about or not? As Professor Joad would say, 'it all depends on what you mean by dignity.' If you mean the assumption of airs and graces by those whose complex is so inferior that they must do something to create an impression, it is neither worth writing nor even thinking about. If you mean nobility of aspect, outlook, personal bearing—then it is certainly worth writing about.

What I personally love about the word is its *astronomical* meaning: *the situation of a planet in which its influence is heightened, or is unusually high*. That is a planet's dignity. What a lovely thought! If our own dignity is to mean our influence is heightened, or is unusually high, because of the situation we find ourselves in—then we deserve every honour that comes our way.

We have only to think of people we have personally met, or who have been in the public eye at various times, to realize how they have attained a dignity of that kind. Such dignity is thoroughly enviable. We have only to think of other people we have known who do not seem to be in that category. Unless personal dignity is absolutely natural, totally unaffected, there is nothing particularly dignified about it. Such dignity is merely a pose, a show of assumed importance.

One of the most charming personalities I ever came into contact with was that of the late Sir Henry Wood. He possessed an enviable charm. Quite early in life he began to cultivate a platform personality. His common sense told him that his back view, which he presented to his audiences, mattered quite as much as his front view, which he presented to his choirs and orchestras. By carefully-rehearsed movements he was not only able to convey by the least gesture what he wanted to convey to those who sang or played under him, but he managed to do the same for everyone sitting in the hall behind him. Consequently their pleasure was heightened because their understanding was heightened. Sir Henry's audiences hardly saw his face until he turned round to receive their applause; when he did that he seemed almost transfigured.

Sir Henry was the only man of my acquaintance who ever dared appear in public wearing a carnation in his evening dress coat; yet there was nothing affected in his doing that. Quite on the contrary, those carnations seemed part of his personality. The batons he used were longer than any I ever saw (I still possess one he gave me) but there was something outstanding in every movement he made with them. He never made a meaningless movement; but I know for a fact (because he told me) that he never made movements in public he had not previously rehearsed in private. Delicacy and accuracy of movement were as much to Sir Henry Wood as to Anna Pavlova.

If you care to visualize —in an analytical frame of mind— the personality of someone you know and admire, you may find that what you have so much admired in that personality has been gradually put together by intensive rehearsal. Personalities are built up; none of us inherits them ready-made. If an actor has to rehearse the personalities he represents on the stage there is no valid reason why you or I should not rehearse in the same way. Personality matters so much. Unless we put our own constantly under review, subject it to close scrutiny, it is likely to play us false.

If our dignity is such that we repel others we must be content to know that we have chalked a mark on the floor— *and that others will see we stand on it.* They will *keep* us standing on it. We are at fault astronomically: our planet is *not* in the ascendancy; its influence is *not* heightened.

If we rehearse badly, or insufficiently, we cannot expect our performance to be anything but shaky. If we rehearse sufficiently, and well, that performance may be so impelling as to be worth all the trouble we have taken with it. We are what our thoughts make us, and if we secretly borrow from other personalities we may be able to repay them by the result in ourselves, even if they know nothing about what we have been doing. They may never know anything has been borrowed; instead, they may borrow something from us. Even if they do we shall never know we have lent it.

Thought-expressions are forces. So much depends on the way they are delivered. If we differ from a friend, or even someone who is not a friend, we need our wits about us if we are to put our point of view in such a manner as to make him not only see it, *but want to see more of it*. If our thought-expressions are so forcefully ejected that we overpower our opponents we engender an unenviable situation. While we are with them they agree with us—or seem to; but the moment our back is turned they have a good deal to say, not much of it to our credit.

We all know people of that kind. While they are with us it seems we *must* take notice of them; as soon as they have gone we wonder why we *ever* took notice of them. Persuading people against their preconceived convictions is usually a poor game to play; but a really attractive personality can often play it and win on points.

Perhaps the greatest danger any of us can run in the building of a personality lies in our falling into the clutches of vogue and fashion. The young maiden who wears a certain style of hat because it is the fashion, and not because it suits her, does little or nothing towards her personal dignity. She does still less when she makes it patent that she has quarrelled with her Maker to such an extent that she has taken it upon herself to remove the eyebrows He gave her, and has substituted two dark lines, both out of drawing and not even a pair. When she colours her lips so that she gives the impression of being in the throes of a heart attack, or when she grows her finger-nails like a falcon's talons and paints them post-office-red, she seems to have lost her last shred of dignity, to have given up life as a human, and to have joined the ranks of Rossum's Universal Robots. Technically, she has committed the atrocious mistake of using stage make-up off stage.

And yet—how great a grace springs from a really beautiful personality, from one who can always be relied upon to behave perfectly in the situation of the moment! How great is the charm of a serious-minded man who can forget to be serious for once in a way, and can fool about without the least loss of dignity!

If you yourself have found your real personality together with its attendant dignity, and yet can relax to amuse others, you do a grand thing. Should it fall to your lot to entertain a baby you need lose nothing by going on all fours and temporarily changing into a big bear. During the process your thought-expressions may have to undergo modification; so long as the baby appreciates your power to characterize, and signifies approval with laudatory gurgles, you need not consider yourself a failure.

Personality is a complex affair. It *must* be, because it is the sum-total of everything about us, our thinking, our inspirations.

Inspirations are odd things when we come to examine them. They are come by in an odd manner. Half our time we fail to recognize a brainwave when one comes our way; it is only when we become used to their arrival that we recognize them. Yet, if we let them, they will come in their thousands. To be sure of them we have to learn the intricate art of letting our minds run into neutral gear.

In doing that there is a definite art; it means clearing the mind of every active thought for the length of the Greenwich Pips; then, if our minds are really trained, thoughts will rush into the empty space we have provided and keep us going splendidly for some time.

When a musician improvises it is a mistake to suppose his improvisation to be instantaneous creation and performance. Improvisation has been wrongly defined that way. The creation and the performance are by no means instantaneous. To improvise at all a player must have harmony and counterpoint at his finger-ends, but if he is really an *improvisateur* his mind is flying ahead of his hands. While he produces sound his audiences hear, he hears sounds he *will be producing* for them in a few seconds' time. His mind is constantly becoming a blank and musical thoughts are rushing in at a terrific speed. That is what happens when a musician improvises. I speak from practical experience.

So it is with the more ordinary things of life. The trained mind is purposely 'blanked' in order that the deeper faculties can take control. Consequently the whole mental outfit is flashing at white heat and top speed.

Inspiration has a sister faculty: intuition. This is—need you doubt it?—part of the power to think, part of your very birthright.

Intuition is no part of the power to *reason*. If it were, it would lose much of its immense value. Intuition comes against the reason as a thunderstorm comes against the wind. When any of us finds we are suddenly conscious of danger, a warning comes as a flash on the ether. How many times has it done so already, and we have been thankful we obeyed it; how many times, alas, have we disobeyed our intuition - and suffered for it!

Intuitive powers were given to us to use; they are, as I have said, part of the power to think. *So that we have had them all along*; but we have had to get used to the fact that intuition is always in a hurry, that it does not act slowly as the reasoning faculties do.

If we train it, our intuitive faculty will often get us out of a hole. We may be asked for an opinion when that opinion, if given truthfully, is going to hurt someone. The intuitive brain acts like a flash, and we say the right thing and use the right inflection for the saying of it. It is not for us to cause our thought-expressions to wound someone else merely because we consider we have a way of speaking the truth. If we are to carry out an honest purpose in life it is obvious that we must make a habit of telling the truth in the broad sense, but particular occasions demand particular treatment. We can always tell the truth in so far

as it does not hurt or cause mental suffering, but there is
little to be said for the often-bragged-of policy of telling
the truth and shaming the devil. The answer to that is that
the devil can do his own shaming; he needs no help from
you or me. I have said this already, but does not philosophy
insist on it?

Intuition, trained, is a force. It is the primary force behind
discernment. Without discernment no-one can get very
far in this world. As the world is what it is, and as the
people in it are what they are, we must be able to read our
fellow-creatures. We have also to remember that mind-
reading thoughts are powerful. It is possible to do damage
with them. If we detect something wrong in someone
else we do that person a bad turn if we allow our powers
of discernment to pierce his mind as an arrow would
pierce his flesh. Expression of countenance is something to
watch; people draw conclusions from such expressions,
which are actually thought-expressions. It does not do to
give too much away.

As a nation, we are not particularly good-looking. In
a way, that may be fortunate because if we were all Adonises
and Venuses personal beauty might be something to regret.
As it is, beauty of face and grace of form are held in esteem.
All the same, have you never seen what you might think
of describing as 'beautiful ugliness'? Perhaps it has been in
some matured priest whose features, viewed critically,
leave most things to be desired but whose beauty of
expression is extremely attractive? No doubt you can call
to mind quite a number of people you know, or even do not
know personally, whose facial expression fascinates you.

It may chance that you have lost sight of an acquaintance
or a friend (for perhaps ten years) and then have suddenly
come upon him. By the ordinary process of thought-
association you rapidly compare him as you now see him
with his appearance as you last remember it. In those ten
years he seems to have 'grown a face'. The lines of it have
deepened; the eyes appear more penetrating; the mouth
curls up in a sweetly whimsical fashion; the hair has
whitened. It may occur to you that such a change must

have come about by the acquisition of spiritual power, though a materialist might be more inclined to regard it as the result of the development of the thyroid gland.

It is often possible to watch and witness really beautiful changes that come over the faces of men and women who have sought and found spiritual power. A materialist will still insist it proves nothing, but that is because most materialists are averse to taking anything for granted. They must have definite proof before they accept anything; but the fact remains that beauty of mind is often vividly reflected in facial expression.

In these modernistic days, when agnosticism is so common and religion not so common, anything with even the least touch of the sanctimonious about it may be held up to ridicule. There are still a few of the 'parsonified' parsons left; they are generally laughed at and not often revered. Their trouble is that most of them need to use a thoroughly good modern polisher; their reflections are too dim to be of much use. They want stronger headlights. We all know it is useless to try to drive fast on sidelights only.

The thought reminds me of an uncle of mine, a confessed agnostic, who was accosted by a pious-looking female in the street. She asked him whether he was 'saved'. His reply, I thought, suited the question.

'Ra-*ther*', he said. 'Last week.'

That woman was a fool. She may have agreed with St Paul's ideas of admonishing one another with psalms and hymns and spiritual songs — but she forgot the age she lived in. Even in these days religion and religious matters can be mentioned, but there is a right and a wrong way of mentioning them. To my agnostically-minded uncle that particular woman was to be pitied for having been, as he picturesquely described it, 'struck with the mission'. Had she been a woman with some power about her, he might have admired her. He might even have listened to what she had to say; but because of her ridiculous attitude he merely laughed at her. He objected to having a spiritual torch flashed in his eyes. Had there been real reflection he would probably have been attracted by it.

These days are modernistic, but there have been *no* days when the John Bull type of bluntness was really admired by anyone whose judgement was sound. He who flatters himself he calls a spade a spade is flattering himself upon part of his own inferiority complex. Saying what one means and meaning what one says is another matter; even so, there is never any need to say anything that hurts. To leave someone braced for our having been with him is to leave what may be called 'virile sympathy.' That in itself is a power.

Sympathy is a magnificent word with a wonderful thought about its meaning. *Pathein* is a Greek verb (the infinitive) meaning *to suffer*. The *sym* part of the English word is a variation of the Greek preposition *sun* which, by the way, is pronounced to rhyme with *tune*. It means *with*. So that *sympathy*, by its etymological meaning, is an attitude of *suffering with* a person who is himself suffering. An extension of that meaning suggests that one helps a person because one's mind suffers *his* suffering *by reflection*.

By scientists the word *sympathy* has long been accepted in the sense of *power*. The simplest example is probably *sympathy of vibration*. It is one of the laws of acoustics.

Have you never heard a church window rattle while the organ is being played? Very low notes on a powerful pedal-stop will often cause what is termed 'a sympathy' in objects about a church.

Perhaps you have seen a singer with a powerful voice perform a parlour-trick with a thin wineglass? Having previously tested its 'note' by rubbing a moistened finger round its rim, the singer has held up the glass, sung the note he produced by the rubbing process, and shattered the glass. Again, sympathy of vibration.

I knew a pianist who always locked his piano when he was not using it. Before he played he took the key out of the lock and laid it on the sconce at the side of the key-board. When he struck treble B flat the key jumped off on to the carpet. Sympathy of vibration again.

You will appreciate that the church window rattled because the pedal-stop (probably an open diapason) caused

one of the notes on the pedal-board to find its mark in the
window above; the singer split the wineglass because the
note he sang (the glass's own note) found a destructive
sympathy in the substance of the glass itself; the piano key
fell on to the carpet because B flat's vibrations were too
much for it. In all three cases sympathy was a *power*.

Sympathy is *always* a power. It is the force of an understanding mind. If we are conscious that someone needs help
the power called 'sympathy' begins to act within us. The
sympathy in the stronger mind (our own at the moment)
grips the output of thought from the weaker mind, and
pulls that mind up a little.[1]

As I hope to prove conclusively in the next chapter,
thoughts are powerful agencies. For this reason, when we
have helped someone who is in need of our sympathy it is
for us to round off the job by sending *further thoughts of
sympathy towards that person*. Thus we make a grand climax
to what we have done.

So powerful are our thoughts that even when we say
'good-bye' to someone as we leave his presence, we bring
down a blessing upon that person, *provided we are conscious
that 'good-bye' is a contraction of 'God-be-with-you'* which,
centuries ago, became something like '*God-be-wi'-ye*', until
(still later) it became '*good-bye*'. If we use that word as a
thought-expression, conscious of its real meaning, we do
something for the person we say it to; but we need never
give away what we have done (so intentionally) by an over-
inflected tone of voice. These things are best done unob-
trusively.

As there is a power of sympathy, so there is an opposite
power called *antipathy*. *Anti*, in Greek, is a preposition
meaning *against*. So that the etymological inference here is
that one's mind is *against*, or *unmindful of*, the suffering of
another person. It is not always easy to avoid antipathetic

[1] By the expression 'weaker mind' only one thing is here meant: a mind
weakened by sorrow or other spiritual disturbance. There is no question of
comparison of brainpower. It is quite conceivable that the sympathy of a
child might vibrate successfully upon the mind and spirit of an aged scholar.
The question of brainpower does not arise.

feeling towards those we are forced to dislike, or even who dislike us. The former, perhaps, are easier to deal with because we may be able to control our real feelings so adroitly that we cease to transmit antipathetic thoughts; we may even substitute those of sympathy, though they may not be quite up to normal strength. With the latter it is not so easy to deal because someone may make it pretty patent that he dislikes us intensely. Even then, though admittedly it is harder, it is possible to adopt a sort of neutral attitude if we cannot manage anything better. Such an attitude brings its own reward: we are not unduly troubled because of the attitude of that person. And, in the broader sense, if we can get so far we shall at least be credited with a reasonable interpretation of *Love your enemies*.

As a power, sympathy rebounds like a boomerang. If we are good enough to offer others the benefit of our most powerful thought-expressions, a response comes from them even though they have not the least idea of what we have done for them. The response is subconscious, but none the less powerful for that. Not everyone may offer a responsive sympathy: the really ungracious are not likely to. Such response may even come from them in time, but we have all learned that it is unwise to expect anything from a pig except his customary and characteristic grunt. Still, even if he grunts, we need not enter into a grunting competition.

The fact that sympathetic power brings a response can be put to a simple test. In a street full of pedestrians we can select the first ten who actually look at us as we pass them. If we keep our features rigid, regarding them with an expression we ourselves would consider forbidding in *them*, they will return something similar. If we make our expression one of pleasantness, and look at the next ten in a kindly fashion, we see an immediate response. By the way, this test needs a little care: it is not a good policy to give the impression we own the world's copyright of the 'eternal grin'.

Thought-expression, as revealed in facial expression, is all very well in its way; but these days are modernistic.

Anything sanctimonious (whether over-benign or over-severe) belongs to the *overrated* Victorian period. Victorian piety was mainly narrowmindedness. Perhaps it can now be affectionately remembered as something which might be suitably symbolized in our best heraldry and preserved in the Victoria and Albert Museum. We have no further use for it.

What we do need is more broadmindedness in our culture: pleasing manners, pleasant looks and pleasant voices, profound reverence where reverence is demanded, and a thoroughly native sense of humour. We were born *in* time; we do well to move along *with* time. We can afford to be humble yet immensely strong in our humility; we can be debonair in our sympathy, unobtrusive in our charity.

Charity, according to one of our proverbs, begins at home. So should sympathy—but there is no earthly reason why it should ever stop there. All the same, the home is the best place for experimental work with it; and, having begun it there, it seems reasonable to continue to practise it there. Love in the home is, after all, as important as anything we can think of.

Where thought-expressions are likely to come into direct conflict with thought-impressions is in the exercise of patience. The very sharpening-up of one's reflexes, the speeding-up of one's critical faculties, may cause any of us a sense of impatience difficult to deal with. People are slow where we want them to be quick, stupid where we want them to be bright, fatuous where we want them to be serious. Instead of dealing with them gently we want to shove them along; instead of leading them we want to clout their heads. Good for us, if our reflexes are as sharp as all that, but definitely bad for them if we show our real feelings. We do them a poor service if we make them feel uncomfortable in, or because of, our presence.

It has been said that patience is a virtue. No-one ever thought it was a vice but – if we really come to think of it—patience is a *cultivated faculty*. Or, at least, it can be made to work very much like one. Patience is a form of love even if it is true that impatience is not a form of hatred. Patience, forbearing, forgiveness, understanding, are all part of the grace of love which is also part of the grace of God.

If our thought-expressions are (so to speak) soaked in patience it is possible to heal another person's spirit; that must be true because it is inconceivable that impatience can heal *anyone's* spirit. To allow thought-expressions of an impatient kind to go forth from one's mind is to release something which will turn again; such consideration is quite apart from the damage done to someone else's mind, which damage may be considerable because it may rouse something in another person he has been trying hard to suppress. We have no more right to damage other people's minds than we have to damage their personal property.

Thought-expressions of love and goodwill invariably bring responsive thoughts from others. At the lowest they bring something better from the pigs of the world than might otherwise be obtained. There are degrees of grunting, even from pigs; some grunts sound charming --those of contentment, for example.

I have already spoken of the conflict between our thought-impressions and our thought-expressions. It is in the home, more often than not, where such clashes take place. To live with an irritable person means to suffer. It is little comfort to suggest that actually the irritable member of the family suffers more than we suffer; all the same, it is the simplest philosophy which tells us that, by our own unswerving patience and goodwill, it is possible to reduce his suffering —and our own. There may be times when we are justified in rising up against such a person; but if we do so we have to remember that our success must be *assured before we begin.* To take a chance on it is useless because failure only makes things worse. Making a satisfactory job of such rising-up needs considerable power.

That love in the home makes that home a haven of peace and contentment hardly needs saying. You yourself must know families whose homes literally breathe an atmosphere of magnificent love. You sense it the very second you enter. You can think of other families where there is no such love. At heart such families may be united, but love remains unexpressed.

You can, again, think of married couples who have been sweethearts all their married lives, whose silver wedding will mean more than their original wedding-day, whose golden wedding will mean more than the other two put together. And you can probably—and sadly—think of other couples who, though apparently happy, never express their love. They miss more than they know. Probably they would tell you their love is too deep for expression. All you can hope for them is that they are speaking the truth.

Love, in married life, thrives on expression: the unfailing courtesy between him and her, the appreciation of things done, the expression of approval and congratulation on the smallest success, the expression of sympathy and encouragement over any little failure. Where such things happen, every day brings a deeper realization of what love in wedlock can really mean. As the days go by there is deeper and still deeper happiness. No wonder, for love *expressed* is part of the blessing of the Great Lover Himself.

Yes; wise are he and she who never forget they are sweethearts. What a lovely word that is—one of the loveliest in our lovely English tongue!

There are cynics who will smile in their cynical way. Many are there who will say: 'it is all very well to talk like that. How many couples remain sweethearts? Look at the divorce list!'

I know; I *have* looked at it. But I still say that if people used their power to think the wrong men would not marry the wrong women. In any case I shall never cease to say that those who begin as sweethearts can go on as sweethearts.

The cynic's retort is: 'It is easy enough to say that!'

Of course it is. It is easy enough to say *anything*. Perhaps, I had better confess that I do find it very, very easy to say that. But then . . . well, you see . . . *I married an angel*.

VI

PROJECTIVE THINKING

THE chief theme of this part of my book.

I do not think I shall begin by apologizing for being so long in reaching it because the power to project can only come to anyone after he has realized what the other forms of thinking (subjective and objective) really signify. I now propose to begin all over again by asking you to consider your position as a creature of God, as a soul-on-earth. If you will also consider yourself to be part of the Divine Scheme-of-Things, you will thereby take the first definite step towards the study of projective thinking, easily the most powerful mental action human beings are capable of.

You are not a marionette. None of us are marionettes. We were not sent into this world attached to strings or wires even though it may in a sense be true that all the world is a stage and we are the players.

We are all here as independent entities with clearly-defined destinies to be master of. Far from bringing nothing into this world, we brought with us a number of hereditary gifts and tendencies; still further from taking nothing out of it, we take the result of *our use of* those gifts and tendencies.

In the worldly sense we are each dependent on each other simply because, alone, it is impossible to feed or clothe ourselves. We must buy from someone; we may even have to sell to someone; we must conform to laws made by someone. So that, in the worldly sense, we can never be said to be in the remotest degree independent.

In the spiritual sense it is altogether a different matter. We are independent entities responsible for our way of life, answerable for our actions and for the influences that flow from us as the result of our thinking, for our attitude of mind, for our very act of living. We are here to make the best of what comes our way.

Yet if that were all it amounted to – if there were no means of lifting ourselves above circumstances and environment, nothing better than a period of existence here made up of work and pleasure, sleep and wakefulness, day' and night, summer and winter—this life would be a sorry affair at the best and certainly of far less account than it really is. We might just as well have *been* marionettes— better if we *had*, for we should have at least relied upon someone else to pull our strings and wires. We could have danced our way through life to someone else's music. Our end here would have been very much like that of a broken toy – but what would it have mattered?

This is our one and only human existence.

Having said that, I fully realize I may be treading on delicate ground. I have no means of knowing your views with regard to the theory of what is generally called *reincarnation*, but having made a definite statement which must be construed *against* that theory I am ready to put a few thoughts before you. I do this with the direct intention of confirming your views if you do *not* believe in reincarnation, and of attempting to alter your views if you *do* believe in it. Unless I succeed in carrying out my purpose I cannot proceed very far with my theme of projective thinking. So here goes.

From the very early days of man's life on earth he has had a notion that some part of him must survive his *death* on earth. Any belief that is ancient is entitled to respect, and this particular belief is very much entitled to respect because it proves that man realized, right from the start, that he was *not* a marionette. As I have already said, man had ideas about his possession of a soul but was hazy as to its real nature.

The cynics laughed. They said man was so infernally conceited that he simply could *not* believe it was possible for him to cease to exist. He believed that he *must* go on because he *wanted* to go on. The worst part about man, according to some of the more cynical cynics, was his egotism.

And yet the cynics were wrong. They refuse to believe it, even now; but the fact remains that man eventually came to believe in his own immortality even if his belief was a trifle shaky; as the centuries passed by he became a little more certain —*but there was always a doubt in his mind.* There were too many varying theories. No-one was quite sure what to believe. And yet the thought of ending in the grave was something man could not quite reconcile himself to; he was convinced that the grave was *not* the end.

Then came the great change in man's fortunes. *The Creator of the world man lived in took the whole matter in hand by sending His Son to furnish incontrovertible proof that man was immortal.*

This was beautifully done. It began by the movement of a star—possibly a kind of comet—to indicate where God's Son was being born as half-man, half-God. It continued by a wonderful life superbly lived, and it ended by a rising from death to prove that death was not the end. Both the resurrection and the ascension were brought about by the action of natural laws; the only difference between Christ's way of leaving this world, and the way we ourselves are allowed to leave it, lies in the fact that his earthly body was united to his spiritual body whereas *our* earthly bodies remain behind while our power to think flashes ahead to receive our spiritual body in the next world instead of in this. The resurrection was a very simple pictorial method of revealing to man what he should expect at death—and, as I say, it was beautifully done.

Even after the passage of nearly two thousand years only one-fifth of the world is what we call christian; but the fact that Christ came here has had the desired effect: man has realized that life does not end on this planet. There may still be human beings who refuse to believe in immortality, but they must form a very small percentage of the two thousand million souls who inhabit this globe.

Long before the coming of Christ man had begun to wonder—now that he had decided he *was* to go on—whether or not he had ever been here before. His thinking was a little immature; but he took the view that, as he *would* go on, he *must* have been here before. After some more thinking he very naturally decided that he *had* been here before, not once but many times. In fact, as far as he could see, he was quite likely to be here again before he became a fully-fledged spirit and took his final place in what he thought of as 'the hereafter'. From all these thoughts rose the theories of reincarnation and regeneration. Both theories are still held by many thinkers. With all due respect to them and their thinking, it is now my definite purpose to explode such theories as belonging to the pre-christian world. *Such theories are pagan.*

Even if you yourself are not a believer in the theory of reincarnation on this earth, you will probably have met others who do believe in it. A woman of my own acquaintance was an ardent believer. She was a kindly soul, and I liked her; but, I honestly think, of all the women I ever met she was the most miserable. Not surprising because she was always saying that she had been here many times before and, for the sins she had committed in her several previous incarnations, she was being punished now. The only advantage I thought she could possibly derive from such thinking was: *she intended to live her present life in such a way as not to run the risk of being sent here again.* From what I knew of her, I honestly think she did try to carry out the highest principles in her life; but she was not a happy woman.

She was immersed in the theory of reincarnation. She never seemed to be tired of talking about it. One evening, as she seemed particularly fluent on the subject, I thought a little inquisition might be diverting. I began by asking her whether she had always believed in the theory of reincarnation. In reply she told me she had read books about it and discussed the subject with friends *seemingly about ten years previously.* That reply made me suspicious for reasons I shall give later.

I next asked her whether she remembered any of her previous incarnations. When did she think she had lived on earth before —and where? I thought it ought to be important for her to know at least something about her former lives if she was being punished now for what she did centuries ago.

I was disappointed to find her so hazy about them. She did, however, tell me she thought she remembered being a man in the time of Henry VIII. I then asked her to tell me about her *first* incarnation, adding that I expected she would know a good deal about that. She cheered me considerably by saying that she could not be expected to remember her earliest incarnation because *all* of us became what we are in this life by means of a long and painful process of evolution. To begin with, she said, we were all animals. Some of us were insects. She herself, she thought, began as a grub. I am bound to say that nearly convinced me because. in some respects, I thought she resembled one; but I naturally kept such irreverent thoughts to myself. All the same, I found it extremely difficult to keep serious.

Not every believer in reincarnation goes so far. More often one finds people inclined to take an agnostic view: they think they *may* have been here before. But my friend allowed everything in her life to depend from the idea. She accepted her worries and troubles because she had deserved them on account of what she did in the time of Henry VIII, or Charles II, or George IV. Consequently she was determined to make this her *last* incarnation. I told her it would be, but she was obviously none too sure. And so she proceeded on her way – unhappy.

It never seemed to occur to her that such a theory insults the creative mind of God. She never got so far as to think that the Almighty is never guilty of false economy. He does not strike a human body with its soul only to turn that soul back again into another body, repeating the process over and over again. A soul so treated might enter a dozen bodies in a thousand years, first male and then female, assuming a dozen different names. At the end of all these repeated lives who *is* the soul in the next world?

Apart from such consideration, can any of us suppose for one moment of time that if we were born in 1900, it is because of our misspent life which began in 1800, or even in 1700?

As I tried to argue with my friend, if we were all born *with the knowledge* that we were here for the second, third, or fourth time—if, as soon as we were conscious of our own beings, we knew *by instinct* that we had been here before, there might be something in it. My friend admitted that she had only been studying the theory *for ten years*; she confessed that she had never even thought about reincarnation as a child. When I pointed out the weakness of the position she replied by saying that the Creator had been good enough to tell her *at last*, so that she could ensure for herself *this time* that she would never be sent here again.

I insisted that no Creator who is a God of love would have allowed her to go through a number of incarnations in ignorance of the real reason. I pointed out that the only possible chance for her would be if she were *told*. I did my utmost to make her see that the theory would be world-wide, that it would be almost the chief topic of conversation among man and his fellows —but she would not listen: she preferred her theory and its attendant misery and hopeless-ness.

I did not go so far as to ask her whether she believed in the further theory that reincarnation is the loss, at death, of one physical body and the getting of another. I could have told her that, according to one writer, when a spirit is tired of the body it inhabits, it can always set about finding another (presumably of some entity unborn) and, *if suc-cessful*, take up its abode there. I could have explained that the process is thought to be a kind of mesmerism—-but I hesitated before upsetting her still more; besides, I was afraid of an unfortunte temptation to be mischievous.

If the theory of reincarnation were founded in fact, if it were really true that we do come back here time after time, it seems a very strange thing that Christ did not say so definitely. Everything else he said was definite enough. All the reincarnationists can find to quote from Christ's say-ings is: 'ye must be born again'. And yet it was quite obvious what Jesus meant by that: death *here* is birth *there*. In that sense we *are all* born again —and that was the sense in which the statement was•meant.

In any event, a single quotation is not enough to found a theory of such immense importance to the human race. If it were a fact that you and I are likely to return to earth to live more than one life the same would have applied to any of Christ's disciples. Jesus explained everything so clearly; it is inconceivable that he would have deliberately omitted all reference to what would have been of tremendous importance to the whole world. He would have warned his friends first, and the crowds who listened to him second, about something that must have occupied his thoughts all the time he was on earth; yet the fact remains that not one word did he utter which can be even remotely construed as having the least bearing on the subject.

The fact that he was never called upon to answer *a direct question* on the subject is accounted for by pointing out that the Jews had no knowledge of, and therefore no belief in, the theory. The nearest any of them ever went was in the question about the woman with the seven husbands —but even then there was no suggestion of reincarnation on this planet.

Christ came on earth for a purpose. The purpose is clear enough. Moreover, he fulfilled that purpose. Had reincarnation been a fact, he would have spent much time in dilating upon the wisdom of avoiding the risk of being sent here again. He would have certainly altered the parable about Dives and Lazarus. He would have pictured Lazarus as being received into his Father's kingdom while Dives would have been pictured as having to come on earth again—perhaps as a richer man still, perhaps only as a poor one.

Christ is the only authority we have ever had on this particular subject. There has never been another. Surely he should have known, considering he was the Son of God? Therefore we may safely conclude that there is no longer sense nor reason in our believing in a thoroughly miserable theory formed by man long before Christ ever came here at all. The theory of reincarnation is pagan. As such it can be regarded —and discarded. Neither you nor I have ever been here before; we shall never be here again.

If you needed convincing, *I hope I have convinced you.*

To return. If you and I are merely to regard ourselves as the creation of our parents and the creators of our children, expected to live in accordance with the rules of such societies as we happen to be members of, there must be something radically wrong with the frequently-quoted statement that God created man a little lower than the angels.

It would be much nearer the truth to say that God merely created man a little higher than the animals. For, after all, the animals are the creations of their parents and the creators of their children; they also conform to the rules of the societies they belong to. Jungle-law would suit them and us equally well.

It cannot be denied that we are all members of some form of society. No-one with a grain of sense would attempt to deny it. Even so, the statement does not mean that you or I are merely cogs in a wheel. We are definitely part of the Divine Scheme, but we need not conclude that we are either robots or automatons.

Far from it, because —by His very office as Creator—our God derives less satisfaction from our presence here if we wander through life without even trying to understand the meaning of it, instead of realizing that we each hold His commission and that it is a matter of courtesy upon our parts (even if nothing better) that we execute that commission faithfully. If we regard life in that way it will certainly have a very definite meaning. We do well to consider ourselves important enough to be here as part of the Divine Scheme; we do better when we think out how to make a good show of our part in that scheme; we do best when we grip the vital truth that, in the doing of it, *we must waste no time.*

Wasting time must be unheard of in a society of saints and angels. Admittedly it is time in eternity where (it might appear) there is enough to waste without mattering very much; but wasting time in this life, where so much has to be crowded into so short a period, should also be unheard of. More loosely expressed, time is stuff to spend, sometimes merely to pass, but always too precious to kill. It dies hard, anyway. It even refuses to wait for a second, its own smallest division.

There is another aspect of time: *our consciousness of it.* Being *un*conscious of time is a low mental state associated with, senility, or even with imbecility. To be vividly conscious of time is *Life*.

Also it is very easy—in these days especially, because everything lies at hand. Big Ben and the Greenwich time-signal, between them, do much to make us all conscious of it.

Some people have no idea of time. They admit it. They can do worse than set about altering what is a regrettable condition of mind. We can all afford to be conscious of time.

Fortunately, in the way of effort, it costs us little. A daily paper will supply most of the information we require. From a perusal of it we can discover what is the moment of sunrise and of sunset, of moonrise and moonset; we can learn the time of dawn and that of dark; we can make mental notes of how much longer (or shorter) today's light is than yesterday's. We can, by a little absorbing rehearsal, soon come to know what time of day it is without reference to a timepiece. We can make accurate observations as to how long it takes us to do this or that; or to walk, cycle, or drive, distances we are in the habit of covering by one or all such means. In fact, *we can become thoroughly conscious of time*.

In his charming fairy play *The Blue Bird* Maurice Maeterlinck makes Time a character. Much as I admire the symbolism of this play, I am doubtful whether Maeterlinck was right in making Time refer to his 'Sister Eternity'. Hardly his sister, surely? So vast is eternity that time can only be the merest incident in it. I fear me that good Father Time's sister must have been a very old lady. Of eternity none of us can ever be even remotely conscious—at least, not while we are still on earth; but we can have thoughts of time surrounding us all our time here, if so we will. It is important that we should.

For this reason. *Time is a power.*

On its journeys round the sun, even this old world of ours has to obey the laws of time. It has to complete that journey in 365 days, 6 hours, 9 minutes, and 9 seconds. Not *ten* seconds: it is more than our world dare do to be a second late. Powerful as must be the forces which send the earth round the sun, time itself is so powerful that it cannot be forced. Not even our great globe, whirling through space at a colossal speed, can make time obey it. Time never gives way. Time's laws never change. No matter how we measure it, time remains time.

When the Almighty Creator made the universe He made time to go along with it. Time is actually part of the Mind of God. Him alone does it serve. In a sense, it must also be true to say that God obeys time because He obeys all His great laws of creation. He must have thought well of time, and the importance of it, because it was not long after man came into this world that God taught him how to measure it.

Because time is part of God's power, the act of becoming conscious of it turns out to be a simple and direct method of becoming conscious of God as the Maker-of-time. It is so easy to become conscious of time, and everything to do with it, that this suggestion becomes eminently practicable. We can always add to our rehearsals by noting anything and everything remotely connected with time ; everything to do with the four seasons of the year; everything to do with the months. Even everything in the way of what we may generally expect in the weather is connected with time—at least, in this part of the globe.

Knowledge of elementary astronomy is of considerable help. It hurts no one to be able to recognize at least the chief constellations, or to know how to identify the Pole Star by drawing an imaginary line from the base of the Plough, up its right-hand flank, stopping at a dull-looking star almost in a direct line above it. Or to let the eye travel on past the Pole Star and recognize five quite brilliant stars known as Cassiopeia. Such knowledge is easily acquired. Astronomy helps enormously; but *astrology* avails us nothing.

Astrology wastes men's time.

Any time we spend on reading what the so-called astrologers say is a gross waste of time that might be better employed. These 'seers' tell us that we were born under this planet or that star; they also tell us what to expect as a result. We can all read the cheap Sunday press and study our future from what we are told; but we shall not miss the rather significant fact that whatever future is in store for *us* is also in store for *everyone else* born on the same day. We can throw all reasoning to the winds and become thoroughly superstitious, fearing to do anything on a Friday, or to sit at a table with twelve other people, or to walk under a ladder, or to break a looking-glass; or even to bring a bunch of 'May' into the house. We can build our lives on some such code, *but we merely waste time*.

If we waste time we waste something that is a power; we waste something that gets its power from God. And there is little to recommend that. As time is part of the Mind of God, the more we become conscious of time the more we become conscious of the Maker-of-time.

I have already established the fact that the soul of man is his power to think. I have also pointed out that Christ, while on earth, was in communication with his Father whenever he chose to be. I further pointed out that there was a technique to that because there is a technique to everything in, and out of, this world. The technique in this particular instance was Christ's power to cause vibrations on a line of ethereal rhythm. The nearest power to it (which *we* know) is what we now call radio transmission. Christ's thoughts were throbs on the ether even though his spoken words may only have been vibrations on the air. As for him, so for us.

And by the laws of God.

Each of us possesses what amounts to a private radio installation, complete with transmitter and receiver. By means of the former we transmit our petitions; by means of the latter we receive our inspirations. I have said all this before, but I say it again as a reminder of something of vital importance.

And now for another thought. The Creator of the world possesses what may be termed *projection of personality*. This power is contained in His omnipotence. It is really another way of saying that, being as He is, the Creator is everywhere at once. A childish way of putting it, perhaps, but it will do. That is what it amounts to, anyway. Projection of personality means that the possessor of it is conscious of the universe as a whole, but also of every thing (animate or inanimate) and every living creature in it.

Such power is not confined to the Godhead alone even though it flows primarily from Him. Christ possesses it; it is invested in the Third Person of the Blessed Trinity. It is, again, given (though possibly in a lesser degree) to the higher Intelligences of the next world — the Angels, if you prefer to call them by that name. I think I do because the Greek word from which our word *angel* is derived means a *messenger*. A charming thought.

It is interesting to note that, while on earth, Christ made infrequent use of this power which he must have possessed in full. Walking on the sea and raising Lazarus from the dead were effected by means of it; failure to descend from the cross was a refusal to use it; but the resurrection and the ascension were both brought about by use of it. Although Christ's power was always strong enough to force nature and negative gravity, it is noteworthy that he often trudged along the hot and dusty roads of Judæa when he was footsore and weary. That was because he never allowed his divinity to affect his humanity.

We ourselves are not given the power of projection of personality. We cannot be in more than one place at the same time, however convenient we might find such a power if we possessed it. All we are allowed to project is our *thoughts*. Them we certainly *can* project. The speed at which they travel is that of light, so that they do not take very long to reach their destination. As we have that power it is for us, merely by becoming conscious of the Source-of-power for one second—the smallest division in time— to ensure His becoming conscious of us. He is not likely to forget, or be unmindful of, you or me if we make no use of this power; but if we want power for our purposes we have a simple means of attracting it.

Power is something we need every moment we are awake. We need it in order to think clearly and accurately; we need it to enable us to judge quickly and fairly. This last thought is contained in that age-old lyric known as the *Veni Creator*, where the writer says: 'enable with perpetual light the dullness of our blinded sight.' (A lovely use of the verb *enable*, which here means *empower*.)

We all need the 'celestial fire' that same poet speaks of. We need such fire for power to radiate about us; we need power to absorb, power to reflect. Is there anything in the whole meaning of life that does *not* require power? If there is, I hope you will write to me and tell me what it is—for I can think of nothing.

Mere experience of life will give us quite a little power. That is only natural. We must indeed be dull if we go through life without picking up something from our experiences. As I have already shown, absorbing the best thought-impressions that come our way does much to build up and extend our experience of life; but if we are content to live that life without making any attempt to draw upon the real source of power, we must just make do with what comes our way. It may be much; it may be little. However much it may prove to be, none of us can afford to neglect the power to *absorb* power which was given us as our birthright. Standing by ourselves, day in day out, is hardly an act of wisdom. Because so many people do it, so many lives are played as though they were losing games.

It is not much fun to awaken to the fact we are failing, that we are becoming enfeebled in advancing years instead of growing stronger and still stronger as those years go by. *The proper place for the climax is at the end.*

It may occur to you to ask whether religion is to be allowed to enter into all this. Of course. No-one who has any religion about him can possibly doubt it; but it is not my purpose in this book to say anything definite about religion. One of my reasons is that I have no means of knowing what your views are. Are you a Catholic, an Anglo-Catholic, a Protestant, or a Nonconformist? Or none of these? How am I to know? For this reason I decline to write one word that shall give you the slightest clue to my own position.

For that matter, I have very little to say about prayer.

What can I say that has not already been said? For my purposes here, I am far more interested in the power to flash the ether *for* power *from* the Source-of-power. If you or I are concentrating on a particular piece of work, we can afford a single second in time to be conscious of time — a glance at the sky is enough; indeed, it is quite a good way — and, before that second has fully passed we can receive an answering flash. With practice, we shall find ourselves dealing in split seconds rather than full seconds, so rapid can flash-and-answer be.

Practice is certainly necessary — but then, without practice no technique worth calling such is even remotely attainable. We only learned our alphabet by practice. The more we practise, the more we experiment with time, the more certain are we of increased technique in anything, no matter what. We can add our prayers to what we do in this way — or we can add what we do to our prayers; it does not much matter which way we regard it.

The actual difference between prayer itself and the consciousness-of-power I have been describing is: prayer, whether uttered aloud or not, is a verbal expression of some kind. Usually it takes the form of a request. Consciousness, in the way I mean, is just a flash on the ether, so rapid that there is no time for words. Such flashes are actually wordless thoughts which are generally the most powerful thoughts. It is quite possible to become so skilled at flashing the ether in this manner that one's own reflexes act like lightning itself. And if *that* is not putting the capital L into Life, I wish someone would tell me what is!

It is a terrific thought. It means that we can never be lonely. We can seek solitude and find we are least alone in it; solitude is something we can seek and revel in when we have found it. Loneliness is another matter altogether; it is something any of us may justifiably learn to dread. But there need never be anything like loneliness if we throb the ether for something better. Enough spiritual power will be flashed back to cheer the loneliest heart. Loneliness and solitude are as far apart as the poles; the two conditions are in no way comparable.

Such power gives us all the ability to make accurate decisions because *most* of the power we flash for has something to do with decisions of the moment. Naturally such power strengthens the mind and the perceptions. Such power is accumulative because the mind is the place where we store what we need for future use.

Such power gives us the ability to deal with awkward situations. That, again, is because we are likely to flash for power when we find ourselves in tight corners. The consequence is that we acquire the *general* power to deal with *all kinds of* situations. We become excellent tacticians.

We all need the power to say the right thing at the right moment; without it we shall never sweeten—nor strengthen—our personalities. We need power to avoid hurting others; without it we are likely to suffer moments of remorse. We all need power to act with kindly courtesy, power to amuse, to comfort, to hearten, to advise, to warn. And we certainly need *much* power to deal with anxiety, foreboding, apprehension.

In fact, it simply means that we need power to make our lives a success. The other state —failure —is no good to any of us. If we are failures, we must either confess the fact or else attempt to blaze a trail of some sort—and that means a display of the inferiority complex. The former is preferable because the said complex can ruin three characters out of four.

The surprising thing about the inferiority complex—about which so much has been written—is that people still think it only applies to those who consider themselves 'no good'. It certainly does include such people; but its wider application embraces the petty-minded, the self-righteous, the easily shocked. The inferiority complex is the prime cause of jealousy, vindictiveness, and often of lack of integrity. As for conceit, it is just another name for the complex. A conceited person (when honest enough to admit anything) knows in his heart that he really is no good, but is determined to convince others that he is better than most.

If any of us suspect that we really have developed any

ourselves as possessing no power at all —*and begin all over
again.*

The approach to the Serene must be humble; but if we
have anything in the way of personal characteristics we are
justifiably proud of, we can be proud and humble at the
same time. If we have conquered any weaknesses we once
possessed we can be proud of the fact; we can mix our
pride with our humility and flash the ether with a high heart.
Our Creator is always interested in our successes; at least
they mean more to Him than our failures.

And if we have scored a success during our day, if we
have found time during that day to be conscious of time
itself and so of its Maker, when at last our watches suggest
that the only time for us now is *bed-time*, we can lay ourselves
down in peace and take our rest, braced in soul and gratified
in mind because some of our time that day has not altogether
passed us by in vain. It is a very simple philosophy that
teaches us to be humble and proud at the same time —humble
because there is still so much to learn, proud because we
have managed to learn even a little.

If you yourself would really like a thought for the end
of your day, perhaps this may appeal to you:

> God Almighty, Source-of-all-power,
> Thou Agelessness,
> Who never began, who never can end!
> Burn thou thy great power into my
>   soul this night that I may rise
>   in the morning full of life for my
>   new day.
> Agelessness, Thou who never began,
> Who never can end. . . .

Yes; agelessness. With the Source-of-all-power time is
not time. Timeless Himself, the Creator of time, He
actually never began. He certainly can never end.

Such is the power you and I have to deal with—an
infinite, illimitable power. Yet, All-majesty though He be,
when we are conscious of Him, very politely He returns the
compliment and becomes conscious of us. We are so important in His cosmic scheme-of-things that each one of us is

at liberty to throb the ethereal line of rhythm which connects our souls with His Mind. We may attract attention whenever we wish; for, unlike some people on earth, the Creator requires no 'previous appointment' to be made.

Courtesy alone demands that we realize our privileged position; such courtesy demands that we do not ignore such privileges. We are earth-souls expected by Him, our Creator, to realize our power to project our thinking.

Apart from which consideration, the effect on our attitude to life is so marked. Everything about us is strengthened. This does not mean that our personalities will forthwith become so overwhelming that our friends will begin to think that a very little of us goes a very long way. We shall not become so self-important that they are likely to get sick of the sight of us. Nothing like that will happen, if only because absorbing such power means absorbing something of a *corrective nature*. In any case, to be successful in the way I have been describing, one has to be in a degree humble; one's humility must be thoroughly debonair. The power we absorb from the Source of it is not likely to let us down; we are far more likely to develop a beautiful personality, an inspiring presence—and a smile attractive enough to charm a duck off a pond.

All the same, such power cannot be effectively wielded unless we do something to train it. We are made that way; we have to do things more than once before we do them well. If such power is not beautifully handled by us it is merely power in name; it would smell as sweet by any other. Absorbing power of that depth is something to avoid unless we are prepared to train it.

Fortunately, it is as easy to train as it is to absorb. In either case we are merely making use of natural laws. We cannot disobey a law of nature without coming off second best. None of us can deliberately defy one of God's laws and expect nothing to happen. It will happen whether we expect it or not. But by using our power to project thoughts at the speed of light, through space—through anything and everything existing *in* space—we are merely bringing one or more of those laws into force. The action involves vibrations on the ether—but that is no more extraordinary than what happens when any of us takes part in a radio transmission from Broadcasting House. The only difference at all is that, when we broadcast, the electrical variations we set in motion are caught by thousands of aerials, and reconverted into terms of ordinary sound through loudspeakers. Thus it is possible for our audiences to understand us.

Projection of thought towards the Throne of Grace involves nothing in the way of reconversion into terms of sound. In fact, sound hardly enters the situation. The complete process of flash-and-return is an *etherial* flash; a flash of forked lightning is no quicker. We are always sure of an answer because natural laws *demand* that an answer shall be flashed back. It comes in the form of power, mental energy, perception, understanding —indeed almost anything we can think of.

Unless we indulge in a little simple calculation, we may miss what it all amounts to. One hundred seconds in a day of, perhaps, sixteen waking hours means something like one five-hundredth part of that day; but it is enough to make that day living and vibrant for us, enough to bring us to the end of it with a sense of satisfaction because of so much accomplished in it, enough to have made such a day worth the living. With practice, the real meaning of enthusiasm becomes apparent. What was once considered dull (but had to be done whether it was dull or not) becomes worth doing for its own sake. Time that used to drag begins to spin along grandly.

The most noticeable effect will be on smaller things rather than bigger – at first. Still, we all realize that if we drop things we should hold there is something the matter with our technique. As that technique improves we become conscious that our brain is driving its way into whatever we are doing, and even the dullest job brightens up. From that very simple point of view it is worth making the experiment; in the extended senses it means the turning of second-class brains into first-class – and *that* alters the whole tenor of life. On the other hand, to be conscious of time with an eye on the nearest clock can only result in our having an uneasy feeling that the clock needs attention: *it must be losing.*

Vivid interest in a piece of work always makes a clock seem to gain. Effort has to be made if increased technique is to result; but in that effort always lies a great, though it may often only be a secret, reward. And, above all, the concentrative life is the grandest life, the happiest, the most fascinating. It is altogether a higher form of life.

In order to obtain, and train, power of this quality an absolutely calm mind is indispensable. The rising of anger to any appreciable extent— the very heightening of colour in one's face— is enough to disrupt contact with the power one is seeking. Something of the kind is likely to happen to any of us, but the disruption need only be temporary; we have to remember that the line connecting our minds with the mind of the Creator is an ethereal line. It is not an Atlantic cable— and it will not stand up to our tempers. Yet, by the laws of nature, the very instant we make an attempt to calm our irritation power flows towards us again as though there had been no break, even if it may take us personally a few moments longer to recover our complete composure. The whole process is so utterly natural that only natural laws can affect it. Even in the most trying circumstances a flash from us will be answered by another, and power will be ours the next second. Storms-in-teacups can always be dealt with by people whose minds are powerful.

Power to ensure serenity of mind is always to be had for the asking— but that is because the Mind of God is always serene. For all that, serenity of mind does not suggest anything slow-moving by nature. Far from it. It is, quite on the contrary, only the really serene mind which is capable of developing accurate speed.

Speed is a relative term. One has only to drive a car along a wide bypass at fifty miles an hour, and compare the experience with that of driving in a narrow lane at fifteen, to realize how relative speed is. Safety at fifty on the bypass is almost assured; danger in the lane at fifteen may be excessive.

Furthermore, there is a great difference between speed and hurry. It is easily defined. Anything done in a hurry means an attempt to do something faster than one's personal technique allows, or else faster than the technique of the job itself allows. Naturally there are times when one is bound to hurry and is compelled to rush something through which, normally, one would take more time over; but that can be regarded as the exception, not the rule. To hurry through work on principle can have only one result: *imperfect execution*. Hurry is one thing, speed quite another— that is, if it is to be *accurate* speed.

Appreciation of what accurate speed really is should come to anyone who watches a great pianist; but he is not a great pianist who plays a movement of a sonata at a greater speed than its composer intended it should be played at. By increasing the speed of that movement the pianist gives a poor account of the composer, even if he manages to show off his own pianistic technique. Accurate speed can only mean one thing: *speed which is accurate for the work in hand*.

For its own sake accurate speed is worth developing — not only in work but in pleasures. In outdoor games not least. The thought reminds me to observe at this point that if you yourself are critical of any suggestion that you should become conscious of the Source-of-all-power merely to improve your service at tennis, or your general prowess on the golf course — *I have an answer for you.*

Why do you play games at all? Primarily, I imagine, for the love of them; but also for the exercise and general enjoyment they provide. Do you not play your games seriously enough to want to play them decently? Do you wish to remain a 'rabbit' all your days? Do you not enjoy trying to beat your opponent? Have you not had a body given you to exercise and take care of? Does not the playing of games come under the heading of relaxation from work? Do you not hope' that such relaxation will make you fitter for that work?

The answers are obvious. And, on glorious summer evenings, when you play your favourite games with friends whose society you enjoy, you can do worse than become conscious of time again—*a time to love*. Surely you recognize that it is often on a tennis court or in a playing field that you reveal your personality at its best; that *is* what we call 'the sporting sense'. Therefore you do nothing unwise, much less undignified, when you allow your mind to flash for a second beyond the beauty that surrounds you, beyond the sound of the wind in the trees, on towards that setting sun—nay, for *half* a second, and—for the other half —*further still*, towards Him who made both sun and sky. An answering flash comes back within a second, and your whole being reaches out over your game and the pleasure you are experiencing.

That is all it amounts to, very often; but if you have learned how to throb the ether successfully, you do something for yourself as well as for those with whom you play your games. You are at liberty to absorb power for everything you undertake; if you are wise you will never be satisfied until your projective thinking is the greatest power about you. All you really need is a vivid consciousness of anything connected with time, knowing that time itself is a power, that the Maker-of-time is the Source-of-all-power.

Even if your work, by its nature, means that one day is very much like another, you will find that (by looking into your day) there has always been something outstanding in it even if only in your thoughts. If you become so conscious of time that a day —because it is a convenient division in time —has really meant something to you, you will find *age* seems very insignificant and what is called 'growing old' very trivial. Instead of thinking in years you think in days. It is one thing to be a year older, quite another to be only a day older.

Such a way of thought does really offer something towards an explanation of what Christ meant by 'taking no thought' for the morrow. Obviously he could not have meant that there is no need for any of us to make preparation for the morrow. By that word *morrow* he meant the *future*; by *taking no thought* he meant *worrying*.

Worry is an intellectual disturbance of a negative type.

Problems occur and recur; they always will. Worrying over them instead of flashing for power to deal with them is, by comparison, a poor action. To give serious thought to things of the future is a sane and sensible action; to worry about them is to act in direct opposition to everything connected with your power-to-think.

In any event, the antidote to worry is the same as that to fear: *faith*. The thought brings up my former point with regard to the absorbing of power: *if we absorb it we must train it*. Even training it will serve us but indifferently unless we have faith in it. We have to remember that if nothing succeeds like success it is also true that nothing fails like failure. In other words—*to him that hath*, etc.

That is part of God's law. Had it not been, Christ would not have made what seems a harsh remark. Its apparent harshness is greatly modified, however, when we amplify it by rendering it in a slightly altered form: 'to him who asks shall be given; but from him who will not ask may be taken more than he can afford to lose.'

If we flash the ether by projecting our thoughts—especially our technical thoughts—with all our strength, that very strength will itself increase. That can only mean we get more and more power because our projections entitle us to it. If you yourself become really clever at using your powers in this way, you will find that you will be prevented from projecting for anything not really good for you. The power in itself is protective; therefore you will not make mistakes of that kind. Moreover, your mind will have become so receptive that your judgement will become completely accurate. *So that you will really believe in yourself*.

Obviously it is useless to ask, and receive—and yet not have faith in what one receives. It is for us all to have faith in ourselves, to keep our complexes thoroughly superior.

Much has been·written about faith. Most of it wrong—at least, so far as my own reading goes. Faith is no mere un-reasoning trust in any body or any thing. Faith always involves knowledge. If your personal faith is in God, you must have found out something about Him. If your faith in

God is a simple faith you are to be congratulated upon keeping something simple which was never intended to be complex. But neither you nor I can possibly have faith in a Deity unless we have *reason* to offer that faith.

An extension of that thought is: if we are to have faith in the power we absorb from the Creator, we must have found out something about ourselves; otherwise we can never believe in it at all. We must know that we have shed all pretence, that we have cast aside all vanities and conceits. We are *who* we are even though we may not now be what, once, we may have pretended we were.

There is, in all this, not the remotest suggestion of being self-satisfied. If we are *that* our complexes are definitely inferior. So inferior are they that we may feel no urge to absorb power—no matter where it may be said to come from. We may even fall into the error of thinking we can go on very well *without* power.

If the complex superior has really gripped us, there will be no negative contemplation of that nature; we shall be humble in the recognition of our own strength. No-one else will even know we *have* recognized it. There is another thought, too: unless we are really humble in soul we shall not ask at the Throne of Grace for power to do anything.

None of us can fence with the Almighty.

A further philosophy is: if we have faith in ourselves and our power we shall naturally possess courage in the more general sense of the term. In these difficult post-war days we all need courage. We need it to make nice decisions for ourselves and others. Making decisions always entails responsibility; we need the kind of courage which is the result of accurate thinking. We need courage to go on alone when someone we love is taken from us; we need courage to accept such loss without resentment. We need courage to face a bully or deal with someone whose honesty we have cause to doubt; we need all our courage and a good deal of faith when we take a certain course in face of opposition.

Yet, being conscious of the Source-of-all-power (and having faith in our own power) gives us all the courage to go on. And, should it be proved that we were right all along (when those who opposed us were so obviously wrong) we shall *not* crow. We shall leave all that to the farmyard gentleman whose crowing technique is better than ours, anyway.

Faith in the power we absorb gives us splendid serenity. That is because we have to make an attempt to keep our minds calm in order to absorb power at all. Having absorbed it means that our initial effort to keep a calm and reasoning mind comes back upon us. Serenity then *itself* becomes a power within us. And a very satisfying power it is. We proceed with our purposes unafraid. If we find we are mistaken—or if anyone shows us we are mistaken—we are quick to realize it: we alter our course accordingly. But we still proceed. If we know we are right we never give up, much less give in. It is only when we realize we are about to make an error that we do either one or the other.

That such power gives us tolerance must seem obvious. It would indeed be a poor thing were it otherwise. Constant and continual attraction of power from the Source of it never yet made an earthly soul narrowminded.

Had there been tolerance there would not have been two major wars in our time. Tolerance must be one of the Creator's chief attributes for, putting it mildly, it is amazing how He puts up with some of us! And yet, when we realize that His Holy Name is blasphemed every hour of the day, that He is cursed for allowing what some of us disapprove of, ought we really to be surprised should He lose patience and teach a few of us a sharp lesson? Fortunately for us, He is not given to doing that. He is a God of tolerance.

Intolerance is one of the most difficult of weaknesses to cure. We may rid ourselves of sloth, of meanness, of inebriety, of unfaithfulness, even of jealousy—and, heaven knows, *that* is hard enough to banish—and yet we can hold on to our intolerant views as though they were something to be proud of.

Intolerance is no virtue. It is, of course, merely another form of the inferiority complex. It comes from an embittered and a narrow vision; from the attitude that if others do not agree with our way of thinking they are wrong, or unworthy, or merely stupid. They may be all three; but even if we are entirely right and they entirely wrong, the moment we become intolerant we begin to lose power. We shall certainly never persuade them to be of our way of thinking. If we are filled to the brim with our own sense of importance we can hardly be as important as we think because we shall not have absorbed enough power to be considered important *at all*.

We can always have the grace to create the impression that the person we are with is the person we *want* to be with. We can all use our personalities in such a way that those whom we meet leave us with a sense of comfort. If anyone feels uncomfortable in our presence it should be on account of his own attitude, not ours. If that is the case, our personalities must be capable of considerable reflection of the light of absorbed power. That kind of light is acceptable to him who once said he was 'the light of the world'.

If our attitude towards others has constantly been reviewed by us during our stay here we shall probably find that, at the end-of-things-here, our Creator is better pleased with our use of His time. If our lives have been periodically brought under close scrutiny *by us who lived those lives*, there will be an appearance of orderliness about them; but if we run the course without ever having paused to review the way we have been spending time, there will be little that can be called orderly; our lives, in picture, will seem more like a wilderness than a cultivated garden.

And there is always the thought that the Creator will Himself review our purposes and methods in this, our only human, existence. We shall none of us escape that; but, if we use our power to think as the Creator meant us to use it, we need never even *want* to escape such a review. The experience should be charming: *the Review of Reviews*.

And that is what projective thinking is all about; that is what its value comes to. Admittedly an advanced form of thinking, its beginnings are simple and direct. It follows a course that nothing can alter because it is held by the laws of nature. There is no limit to the mental power that may be absorbed in this way; there is no limit to the technique which can be gained in this way. It is by the laws of nature that you and I can project our complete thinking from this world into the next and thus link the life we live with the life we *shall* live. And, in the doing of it, *must* lie peace of mind.

And yet, in our devotion to simple things and simple principles, we can all remain babies even while endeavouring to do a little growing up. Adding to our knowledge and scholarship should be according to our inclinations because, in one short human existence, there is not time to learn everything or even half everything. Even in eternity there will not be time enough to do that.

It all comes back to this simple question of *time*. How important time is! Ecclesiastes said there was a time and a season for everything under heaven. He was right: there is. Of all the times we spend, the most beautiful are the times we spend in loving. If they are to be the chief and most important in our lives there will be precious little time left for hating.

In our simple philosophy we can always go back in thought to our baby days when someone asks *us* the time. We may be able to give an accurate reply after consulting a watch, but the asking may send us back in thought. It may even send us back far enough to make us recall our own earliest days when, as babies, time really meant very little. In those days, when we asked the time we did not even know what we were asking for; we certainly were not interested in the correct answer. Time, in those days, meant nothing. We did not understand what it was. And yet we loved to hear the question answered as we considered it should be answered—in fact, *there was only one way* of answering it to suit our baby minds.

'What is the time?' we asked.

And in the answer, though we did not know it then, lay a whole world of lovely wisdom a simple philosophy:

'It is half-past kissing-time; time to kiss again.'

VII

PEACEFUL THINKING

PEACE does not lie in this world. That has been said many times. Unfortunately, it is true. Perhaps it has not lain there ever since those far-off days when a bright star shone over a farmhouse stable. If the Son of God ever actually thought of himself as the Prince of Peace it must have made his heart ache to have to admit that even he did not come into this world to leave peace behind him. He must have realized that some of the bitterest conflicts man would know would take place on account of his having come here.

We have all read that an angel proclaimed that coming by saying: *peace on earth, good will towards men.* That, at least, is what we have been told.

Did Gabriel actually say that? Or is the translation incorrect? May I ask you to construe this: *Gloria in excelsis Deo* . . . Glory to God in the highest; *et in terra pax* . . . and in earth peace; *hominibus bonae voluntatis* . . . to men of good will.

That is not the same thing. And there is reason to think that the Latin version is the oldest and the only correct version. *That* is what Gabriel said: *to men of good will*, not *good will towards men*. It is just as true to-day as it was that night nearly two thousand years ago.

Perhaps the thought of peaceful thinking, and of seeking a tranquil mind, has reminded you of the words of Mendelssohn's well-known and lovely motet *Hear my prayer.* If it has, you will be thinking of 'O, for the wings, for the wings of a dove! Far away would I rove; in the wilderness build me a nest, and remain there for ever at rest.'

Lovely as are those words, lovely as is the music which sets them, there is no philosophy behind them. Many of us have heard them sung --some of us may have actually sung them—but we never extracted from them anything except æsthetic pleasure. To seek our own private wilderness, to shut ourselves away from the world with its cruelties, its backbitings, its bickerings, its blasphemies, is no way to find peace. Far more likely are we to find the real difference between loneliness and solitude by mistaking one for the other.

Peaceful thinking is something to add to our more forceful subjective, objective, and projective thinking. Indeed, these three forms of thinking are not complete without the addition of peaceful thinking. Our worries are usually with us, as are our problems; but if we adopt the attitude that we shall know no peace until we have settled *both*, we go right off the rails in the philosophical sense. Even though our courage is to be admired, philosophy teaches us that we must tackle our worries and our problems *thinking peacefully the while*.

A peaceful mind, if it be a mind practised in thought-projection, is always a powerful mind. The *converse* is true, anyway: no mind that is disturbed is in a powerful condition. It is a mind in a rough state; the thoughts emanating from it are roughened. Turbulent thoughts are always weakened in the struggle to keep themselves steady.

Yet it is a grave mistake in philosophy to imagine that peaceful thinking is sleepy thinking. The whole conception of thinking peacefully lies in uniting it with drive and movement. Far too many of us are disposed to consider drive and movement to be opposed to peace. In philosophy they are by no means opposed. Peaceful thinking and subjective thinking are really inseparable because subjective thinking is about one's personality in the intimate sense. To think subjectively without thinking peacefully is rather like stabbing one's conscience in order to prevent it from doing its own stabbing.

Peaceful thinking must be united with objective thinking because thoughts are so powerful where other people are concerned that, unless a sense of peace pervades those thoughts, one's personality is likely to give the impression that all the fresh air is being sucked out of the room. As for peaceful thinking and projective thinking, all hope of powerful projection is out of the question unless one's mind is calm.

The whole point about peaceful thinking, viewed in this light, is: *it is itself* a power. It grows with the actual power to think. To translate that into ordinary terms means to say that the soul-at-peace is the controlling power of life itself. Peace opposes nothing, but it can be made to surround everything.

Yet a peaceful mind is never in a state of stagnation. Peaceful thinking means continual contact with the Serene Mind. The Mind of God is ever serene, but the serenity of a Creator's Mind must ever be an agency for movement. If our own virile thinking is going to be too much for us, it can only be because we have temporarily mislaid our sense of calm. The sooner we find it the sooner our drive and movement will cease to excite us unduly.

Peaceful thinking *is* a power; it is powerful enough to hold together the other three forms of thinking. Until we can produce the power of peaceful thinking, our minds are likely to suffer from overheating. A delicate machine like the mind will stand any amount of fair wear and tear; what it will *not* stand is *un*fair wear and tear.

That peaceful thinking is primarily acquired by believing in ourselves is capable of easy proof. We have all said at some time or other: 'Leave that to me. I can do it quite easily.'

Only a calm mind produces thoughts of that description. That *is* believing in one's self. The fact that we know we can do a certain piece of work is enough: our minds are not disturbed. That *is* peaceful thinking in one of its most useful forms. It is pure philosophy to extend that thought and apply it to life, and to say: 'To think peacefully while tackling a problem is to be certain of a successful solution of that problem.' In fullest extension it comes to tackling all problems with one's mind in full drive with one's superiority complex set high.

Far too many people hurl themselves at their problems. Success makes them hurl themselves again and again at their problems. Men in the world of commerce will tell us that this is the way to success. It is one way, no doubt; but the result is unfair wear and tear to the power to think and everything connected with it.

I once stayed in a hotel in company with an excellent specimen of a self-made man. I vividly recall his extraordinary abrupt way of expressing himself. His joviality was the joviality of a polar bear. He left out the aitches in most words he was required by philologists to sound them; he applied aspirates to ordinary vowel-sounds with enough force, I thought, to blow up the spare wheel of his car.

His ambition was a consuming fire. I judged that from his conversation, which was all about money. Before I left I knew how much he had paid for at least a third of his wife's clothing. I knew what his son's education cost him. I also received hints as how to invest more money than I have ever possessed.

I used to amuse myself by watching him tackle each newcomer in turn. He talked 'money' to everyone who came into the hotel lounge, and he earned the pseudonym of 'Monty Carlo'. Perhaps I had better confess that I was responsible for that but, as I explained at the time, I thought he must be the son of the man who broke the bank there.

That man missed the whole meaning of life. He had more money than he could reasonably spend—and he spent freely enough—but his mind was never at rest for a second. He told me he detested holidays, but that he had to come away 'just to please the wife'. Holidays, he assured me, were a mistake. They just interfered with business. He hated being at the sea. He only wanted to be where the money was.

He went so far as to admit to me that his doctor had warned him of the consequences to his health unless he took a rest; but rest was something he had missed so far. He had never thought what the word signified. To relax in any shape or form was simply more than he could do. Day in, day out, he fretted because he had another three weeks to waste in this 'infernal place'. It never occurred to him to walk the shore, or to play golf on the links, or to go with his family for a picnic.

This man interested me so much that I actually persuaded

him to go with me for a walk over the cliffs nearby. I thought I would *make* him relax. I had quite a lot to point out to him on the way, but I honestly think he never heard a word. On the way back he turned the tables on me. I learnt more about finance in three miles than I have ever learnt since.

I never managed to get him out again. All he did during the rest of my stay was to sit in the lounge and read the *Financial Times*. The day before I actually did leave I asked his wife where he was, as I had understood from his daughter that they were staying on a little longer. His wife told me he had been compelled to go back to London on urgent business, but the expression on her face as she said that made me think she did not believe him.

To that man peaceful thinking meant nothing. He merely wanted to hurl himself into the world of commerce and show his associates that he was a person to reckon with. I know that because he actually said so, almost in as many words. His whole attitude gave me the impression that his inferiority complex hung on to his superiority complex; it never occurred to him to wrench them apart and begin again. I also gathered that his one thought was of how much money he could leave his family. A man's value—he actually said this—lay in what he was worth when he died. He missed the fact that he was dead already in any sense that really mattered.

I think even his wife thought that. She looked very wistful at times; but it was obvious that it was more than she dared to say what she thought. All I ever heard her do was to protest that he was smoking too much. That was when he lighted a cigar long enough to use as a baton to conduct a symphony orchestra.

And so a living man was dead to the thought of peace. He could never be happy to take today as it was, to spend it without thinking all the time that today mattered only a little, that tomorrow alone mattered. He was never content to absorb beauty from the surroundings—which were extremely beautiful, by the way; he could never enjoy the act of living.

H

His was not the contented mind that realizes the present. How vitally important such realization is! If we are continually recalling what we now consider to be 'the good old days', we had better try to remember whether we *knew* they were good days. We may talk enough about them now; we may sigh reminiscently and compare them with these days which (according to our comparison) are nothing like as good. But did we realize the excellence of those days when we were actually living them? Did we flash our thanks to the Ancient of Days because we were so happy and contented? Or did we let them slip by and, years afterwards, live them again in thought merely to compare them favourably with these *less* pleasant days?

Peaceful thinking *always* embraces the present. This day: it is important *because we are living it*. Do we appreciate the present? Or do we merely remember the jam we had yesterday, look forward to the jam we hope we shall have tomorrow, but loudly bewail the absence of jam today. And when tomorrow comes, shall we begin all over again? Shall we insist that we *did* have jam yesterday? If we do, we are forgetting that this 'yesterday' is now actually *today*, and that we have already been saying we have had *no* jam today.

It all comes to this: we do not know jam when we see it.

The final thought must be that we seek peace and ensue it. If we think peaceful thoughts we are bound to radiate peace round us. If we ensue peace in our own intimate surroundings we shall, in time, affect those near to us who seem to prefer war.

Incidentally, have you ever noticed that people who are always on the offensive often reflect their attitude through their pets? I have known quite a number of instances: a particular case comes to my mind at the moment.

I knew a married couple who snapped and snarled at one another as a kind of policy. Or so it seemed. I do remember that to go to their house was a hazardous proceeding because one never knew whether or not they would be on speaking terms. If they were, which did happen occasionally, they belittled each other in a way that made one feel ill at ease.

They had a dog who agreed with their policy. Every time the bell rang he had to be shut in the kitchen, and he had in his time fought every other dog in the neighbourhood. In the end there was a complaint and he had to be destroyed. His successor was an attractive little puppy, all smiles and creases, but he grew up into a snarling little beast whom it was impossible to make a pet of. I always felt that those two animals reflected the general atmosphere of what might have been a happy home had its occupants produced a peaceful thought now and then.

And yet, in homes where there is peace, its presence is often revealed in the pets of the house. Animals are intuitive; they are quick to appreciate their surroundings. When we think of the trust an animal puts in us –and when we remember he has no soul to take him on into eternity, as we have, we do something for our own souls if we are really all he, in his way, thinks we are.

In Maeterlinck's *Blue Bird* Tylo is Tyltyl's dog who follows him all through his journeys in Fairyland. At the end of the play, when Tyltyl's year is up and he must return to his earthly life, poor Tylo is distressed. He is conscious of his shortcomings, but he is faithful to Tyltyl and promises all manner of reforms for the future, if only Tyltyl will take him back to earth.

'I will always be good! I will never steal in the kitchen again, my little god . . . never steal in the kitchen again.'

But Tyltyl has to return to earth without Tylo, and the faithful animal dies of a broken heart. It is a moving incident in the play, which is full of charming symbolism. It seems that you and I can always afford to be a god to an animal.

Peace of mind has to be sought for because there is so little peace in the world. Indeed, what is there outside our own thoughts? We, however, have it well within our power to create peace for ourselves and for others by good use of our thinking. Practice is necessary for the same old reason: there is a technique to everything affecting us humans. If we rehearse our peaceful thinking, peace will never be far away from us. If you yourself would like

something to say last thing at night, I can think of a verse
of one of the psalms and also a line from one of the sen-
tences in compline. Paraphrased and combined, they make
this:

> I lay myself down now, O God, in peace and gratitude
> for my day, to take my rest knowing that it is thou, Lord,
> only who makest me—and all those I love and who love
> me—to dwell in safety. Be with me, O God, waking; guard
> me sleeping; that, awake, I may work apace and, asleep, I
> may rest in peace.

To seek peace of mind by means of peaceful thinking is,
sooner or later, to find it; and there is nothing on God's
earth equal to it in value. Whether you be high or low in
the worldly sense, if you have peace of mind you are—in the
only sense that really matters—richer than Crœsus himself.

Which thought reminds me of the story of King Midas,
the legendary king of Phrygia. You may remember how
Silenus, a friend of the god Bacchus, promised Midas anything he should ask for in return for a favour the king had
previously done him. Midas asked that everything he
touched might turn to gold.

'That is a fool's wish,' commented Silenus. 'But, as you
ask it, you shall have your request. Everything you touch
shall turn to gold.'

Midas thanked Silenus and returned to his palace. As it
came into view he quickened his steps in anticipation of the
new joy to be his. He would soon be the richest man in the
world. He would spend the rest of the day touching everything in his palace; he would touch every stone it was built
of. He would stand on a golden ladder to do so.

For the next few hours Midas enjoyed himself immensely.
Everything he touched instantly turned to gold. He was
particularly thrilled when he saw his maidservants sweeping
up golden dust into golden pans with golden brooms.
That really did thrill his discontented heart.

When he was tired he ordered a meal, and knew yet
another thrill when he sat down to it. He was about to eat
off golden plates and drink his wine from golden goblets.

He filled a goblet and lifted it to his lips to drink his own health and happiness. His enthusiasm for gold underwent some modification the next moment because the wine and the goblet became one solid piece of gold.

Midas felt his blood freeze. Here was he, king of all Phrygia, the richest monarch in all the world, compelled to starve to death. The poorest peasant in all his realm was richer by comparison. He rushed out of the palace and tried to find Silenus, but no-one seemed to know where he had gone. Then some of his courtiers said they had seen Bacchus in a wood some distance away. Midas went to the wood and (when almost exhausted with hunger and thirst) found the god but, as usual, in an advanced state of intoxication. After much explanation, which Bacchus took in very slowly, Midas managed to make him understand what he wanted of him.

'Very well', said Bacchus at last. 'We gods do not usually take back our gifts to mortals; but in this instance, as you have been good to my old friend Silenus, I might consider it. Go and bathe in the river Pactolus. The curse of the golden touch will then leave you.'

Midas thanked him and did as he had been bidden. The curse left him; from that time onwards the river Pactolus was noted for the gold in its sands.

Midas returned to his palace a sadder but a wiser man. He no longer sighed to be the richest man in the world. He had learned his lesson—and yet, perhaps, not fully learned it. As his palace came into sight he privately congratulated himself that his indiscretion was now a thing of the past. No-one would ever know. What he had turned into gold would remain gold. Altogether it had been a near thing; he had had an extremely fortunate escape. The great thing now was to have a meal and enjoy it. This he did. He then retired to bed after once more inspecting the golden furniture in his room.

The next morning he awoke and lay in bed admiring the beauty round him. His mirror, now of polished gold, attracted him in particular. He got out of bed and went across to look into it. Then his heart missed a beat. To his utter shame and horror, he found that his own ears had been replaced by those of an ass.

From that hour King Midas nursed his dreadful secret. He wore a large Phrygian cap to cover up his shocking deformity. Only one person ever knew: the court barber. He *had* to know, but Midas commanded him to hold his tongue on pain of instant death. The poor fellow did his best, but that secret worried him night and day. Fearing the consequences of divulging it to any living person, the barber dug a hole in the ground and whispered the secret into it: *King Midas has the ears of an ass.* He then covered up the hole and went back to the palace.

As it happened, there were seeds in that ground. They heard what the barber had whispered. Later, reeds grew up. They, also, knew the secret. As they rustled and swayed, they told it to the four winds. And so the whole world knew what the monarch of Phrygia still supposed was his secret: 'King Midas has the ears of an ass.'

That is a grand story. Another version says that Midas was called upon to judge between Pan and Apollo as musicians. Midas decided for Pan. Apollo, in revenge, changed the King's ears into those of an ass. All of which would seem to prove that Apollo, even though he was god of the sun and of music at the same time, possessed the inferiority complex. Perhaps most of the pagan gods possessed it? But the other version is the story of a monarch who had everything *except a tranquil mind.* What was true of Midas is true of many people in these days. Yet there is peace if one seeks it: peace in the meadows and valleys, in the west wind, in the salt air of the sea. Only man is not at peace.

If you yourself understand peace and peaceful thinking, you understand something Midas never understood. You cannot understand the peace of God because it is known to pass all human understanding; but you can feel the power of it when you wish to. It will pervade your senses before you sleep; and in the morning you will awake with a sense of peace for the day to come, a day in which it will be your pride and your privilege to exercise your utmost power. There is another day . . . *to be lived.*

The sea is a music of strings in the dawn,
And the sound of a gannet's grey wings is borne
On the tide.

The birth of a day has brought peace to me,
And my power is ever my pride . . .

A music of strings is the sound of God's sea;
The melodies there are prayers for me. . . .

*   *   *   *   *

And now will you read on? Will you be content to go deeply into a study of the Superiority Complex? Will you make the experiment I have tried to set clearly before you? Will you believe me when I tell you that a tranquil mind will come to you in spite of environment, criticism, ill-health, disappointment, regrets--in spite of a world *not* at peace? It will come to you through contemplation and study, through the power of your own personality, through the power of love--if your complex is superior.

I hope I have not been *too* long in coming to my theme, but I think you will now appreciate how impossible it is to make a study of tranquillity as an attainment in life without having gone back to first principles in order to make the fullest use of what is your birthright . . .

And the birth of each day shall bring peace to you;
Your power shall be ever your pride. . . .

VIII

A TRANQUIL MIND IN SPITE OF ENVIRONMENT

HAVE you ever watched a dancer on a stage plunged into darkness except for a spotlight illuminating the dancer? If you have, you will remember that the dancer moved in a circular patch of light. Wherever he went, the light also went.

Although not in common use, there is a verb *to environ* which means *to encircle* or *to enclose by a ring*. In the passive it means *to be* surrounded or encircled.

So that your dancer was *environed*. The patch of light was the circle in which he moved. The environs of a town or city include all that surrounds them: suburbs, or any out-lying districts. Our own personal environment is primarily our state of being environed or surrounded, but the term applies more especially to the conditions in which we find ourselves and are developed. More conclusively: *the influences about us*.

Influences matter. An influence is something that is influent—something that is *flowing in* all the time; and who of us can afford to ignore what is continually flowing in towards us? Neither shall we want to; but if we are so flinty that no influences touch us we are going to miss things we can hardly afford to miss.

If, on the other hand, we are so pliant that we can be bent this way and that, ruled by every influence that comes our way, we are likely to have a bad time of it. Peace of mind will be out of the question because allowing those round us to do our thinking for us, and so order our lives, is a poor way of securing it—even if it can be secured that way. If we let others make our decisions while we con-tentedly switch off our mental engine, the day will come when the power to think –the immortal soul within us all—will remind us that our 'engine' has not been running in gear lately and that we have seemingly forgotten (or else did not realize) that our power to think is the one real link connecting us with our Maker. Once that happens, we shall know no peace of mind until that engine is working again; and the longer we have left it 'just running' the greater difficulty shall we have in restarting it. The human mind *is* an engine—or, at least, it works very much like one. It must be treated accordingly.

So there is nothing to be gained from slackness of mind, from shirking responsibility, from allowing others to do our thinking for us. We were not sent into this world to be parasites, to depend on others for every mental decision. So long as health is such that we are in full command of our faculties, we are expected to be masters of (not servants to) our individual destinies. We are, each of us, cast for a part, on the world's stage; there is considerable difference between playing a part and understudying someone else's part.

Now it may so chance that you personally have found tranquillity, not in spite of, but *because* of your environment. If so, you are indeed fortunate. If you live and work with others in complete accord and agreement, if nothing they say or do tends to upset the equanimity of your being, if there are no dissatisfactions, no quarrels, no tempers to put up with, you can read this chapter and say: 'none of this applies to me.' You can then do worse than thank God for it.

But, for most people, this is not the case. Environment means so much—and environment is not always what it might be.

Taking the place before the people, the environment of any of us may be the reverse of beautiful. For reasons entirely out of our control we may live in surroundings wholly uncongenial. We may have to live in a town when we should love to be in the country; we may be vegetating in rural surroundings when we should so much prefer the life and liveliness of a city; we may long to be within sight and sound of the sea.

After all, we have only one life on this earth to live. So that we have every right to desire to live our one human life somewhere pleasing; we are certainly to be forgiven for a little wishful thinking. We can all have that 'one day' (in our mind's eye) when we may be allowed to live 'happily ever after'. All the best fairy stories we have known ended that way, and there is nothing in philosophy that can be quoted in condemnation of such a way of thinking.

To be discontented, on the other hand, is a very different state of mind. It is so easy to be dissatisfied. The very development of the critical faculties—so frequently an asset of high value—can be responsible for a discontented and dissatisfied state of mind; but if we allow such a state to exist permanently we merely allow influences to seep through and spoil everything.

Dissatisfaction, obviously the opposite condition to that

of satisfaction, is indeed a negative term. Anything that satisfies us *does enough* for us. The Latin verb *satisfacere* was originally two words: *satis* (enough) and *facere* (to do). Dissatisfaction does not do *nearly* enough for us.

The question therefore is: are we going to let our surroundings saturate our thoughts, as a polluted stream might, or are we going to keep our minds high and dry above their reach?

Our surroundings must in some degree be dear to us. Is there *nothing* right about them? Or is it that we are too fond of thinking about everything we dislike or even hate about them? And if so, have we never thought of counting our blessings? Surely there must *be* some? Is the balance-sheet *all* on the debit side?

Are we ourselves at fault in any way? We might do worse than inquire. If the hole we live in happens to be round, *how square are we?*

If we really seek a tranquil mind in spite of geographical or topographical surroundings, we must at least try to discover how adaptable or unadaptable we are. If our irritations are going to make us chafe day and night we must alternate between two courses: either we must set about altering the conditions or else altering our attitude towards them.

It is nearly always possible to deal with irritations successfully: first, by not talking about them, second by not thinking about them more than is avoidable.

'My father used to grumble about that every day of his life', I once heard someone say. It has occurred to me since that he must have known little tranquillity. He must have added daily to his irritations through laying heavy stress in the wrong place. He would have done better to have accepted what he could not alter, and to have altered what he *could* alter.

That is my first point. Kicking against pricks is a poor philosophy; Christ himself warned us against the futility of it. In extension, Christ's warning suggests that by making the necessary mental adjustments the pricks can be avoided in the sense that we can accustom ourselves to much we originally resented. A further extension of it suggests that if we make the object of our irritation *the subject of our conversation*, a tranquil mind is simply unattainable. Philosophy teaches us that we must refuse to allow our environment to taint our thinking.

Life, for so many, means being environed either at home or at work. We may live our home-lives in beautiful surroundings and have to work in surroundings anything but beautiful; we may do the opposite and prefer the scenes of our work to those of our home. Again, both may be pleasing, or both may be the reverse. If the former, we can count ourselves lucky; if the latter, we shall have something to tackle before we can count ourselves anything like lucky.

If you or I really are square pegs that never fit round holes, and if no amount of planing down the corners of our squareness serves any purpose, our lot is indeed hard; but before either of us finally comes to that conclusion we should be quite certain that some of the edges cannot be treated. It is surely the simplest philosophy in life that teaches you and me to make at least *some* attempt to adapt ourselves to our surroundings. Being a square peg is rather *obvious*. It is an immediate admission of failure. There is something undignified about it.

A trifle futile, too. You must know quite a number of people who go about with their tails down. They usually tell you they never know what it *is* to feel well. It is the weather, they say, which upsets them. All this rain or snow or fog—or else this unbearable heat. A tranquil mind is never theirs, but one wonders whether some of them even realize it: they have not progressed far enough. They are, for the most part, just dragging through life, just grumbling their way through it—through what *might* be so stimulating and enlivening. As we say in colloquial speech, they are 'dead from the waist upwards'. They suffer from, rather than benefit by, most of the influences that come their way.

Yet influences mean everything. Without influences society (as we know it) could barely exist. We all influence each other, but we are all influenced by each other in some degree. The basic idea in the very word is *flowing*, and the inference is: much that flows is capable of flowing in more than one direction. It is the intimate surroundings—the sticks of furniture we live with, the walls, the ceilings, the carpets, the food we eat, that go towards making up the influences which affect us most; and, of course, the general effect of our particular corner of the world. Taken as a whole, the world is a lovely place; it is the people in it who are not all quite so lovely. Most of us know what it is to have dealings with the unlovely people of our own bit of the world.

Yet, if our environment is such that we come into hourly contact with people whose attitude appears to be one of hostility, it is not at all a bad idea to examine our attitude towards them. Allowing ourselves the benefit of any possible doubt, and (for the moment) laying the entire blame on them, our simplest and most effective philosophy is to analyse our own attitude before we proceed to analyse theirs. It may be their offhandedness, their irritability, their arrogance, even their positive dishonesty that is the cause of our own resentment – but how are we handling the situation? Are we so offended at their attitude as to make us ready for them the moment we set eyes on them? Have we already allowed them to see that we are offended, or angered, or merely unhappy? If we have, we have made our first mistake.

I have said this before, but I repeat it because it proves that we have allowed torturing thoughts to banish every chance of a tranquil mind.

Philosophically, we have been at fault because we have (at least, temporarily) forgotten that no-one is wholly bad; we may have even gone so far as to deny the existence of good qualities because of the bad we have detected in such people. If we have to be in contact with people we find it difficult to remain at peace with, and keep conscious only of what we have learned to dislike in them, we shall not make much headway. As time goes on we shall make still less.

If, on the other hand, we look discernedly into the souls

of such people we shall discover good qualities somewhere. If we think more of those qualities than of the others *the power of our thoughts* will have an effect upon those people. If we can go still further and restrain our every feeling of anger or disdain until we have contrived to regard such people with a liking for the good in them, slowly—it may be very slowly at first—we shall begin to turn the balance of their attitude towards us. It may be a slow process, but eventually our encouragement of the good, and discouragement of the bad, will be noticeable.

This is easily proved because the opposite is so obviously true. If we take the other attitude and fight our man every inch of the way, he will surely notice it. Victory may be ours, even so; but it is a poor victory—one that certainly deserves no triumphant celebration.

It is not always easy to smile when we really want to frown, to return a quiet answer (or no answer at all) when provoked beyond endurance; but every time we do it effectively we gain spiritual power.

And that is by no means to be despised. Far from it, because each small gain adds up to one great gain until, spiritually, we win a campaign. We can, figuratively speaking, put up a ribbon. That ribbon, as a piece of philosophical heraldry, emblazons the soul within us; it signifies that we have really made use of our power to think. It is a case of seeking peace and ensuing it. Actually it is a kind of spiritual technique—but then, everything affecting us humans is a technique of some sort or other. And, as nothing in the way of technique comes (or is improved) unless by study and practice, the more one practises the sooner the technique is acquired. The best place to practise in, often enough—is the home—especially if there are people in it suitable to practise on.

In saying all this, I remind you, it was supposed that you and I had the benefit of all doubts—that the blame lay on 'the other fellow'. For a change, we can suppose what is generally true—that there are faults on both sides. If we are really seeking a tranquil mind, we go wrong philosophically the moment we ourselves are guilty of disturbing the peace of someone else's mind. If others are afraid to mention this or that, or to do something else, merely because we are likely to fly into a tantrum about it—or, as was said of Judge Jeffreys—to 'sit down and go into a chafe' (that expression amuses me intensely) we are definitely the cause of disturbance in their minds. By all spiritual laws that affect us, if we disturb the peace of others we may not expect peace for ourselves. To have a tranquil mind we must be at peace with other men's minds. The opposite condition of peace is war, and a warring temperament rarely knows the meaning of peace.

Yet, in spite of environment, it is within the power of all of us to obtain peace of mind by keeping peace round us. It may be 'peace at all costs' and the costs may be appallingly high; but the power of a peaceful personality is such that costs of that kind can be brought down in time, until they eventually become (to all intents and purposes) negligible.

So much for environment. Now for what might be loosely termed our *environs*—our social circle of friends and acquaintances generally. Perhaps the first and most obvious thing to remark on about friendship is that our friends love us in spite of our faults, and that we love them with like reservations. The next thing to note is that our acquaintances are always important because, one day, they may be our friends. Old friends were once new friends; before that they were, as we say, 'mere acquaintances'; before that again, they were either strangers or entirely unknown to us.

Our personal environs are like the environs of a city in that they include all sorts and kinds. They include buildings and districts of varying importance. The most important people in our environed circle must be our nearest and dearest—whoever they may be; the others are ranged according to where they stand in our respect and affection. But, although they each take the precedence over the next-in-order, our attitude towards them collectively is mistaken unless we accord the least important among them the same courtesy (though not necessarily the same

Intimacy) as we extend towards friends of longer standing.
if our minds are above all suggestion of the complex
inferior we shall waste no time in trying to impress them
with what we consider to be our personal importance;
if we really *are* important we can leave the matter in their
hands. We need not upset our balance or poise in seeking
to establish something that can be left to establish itself.

On the other hand, nothing is to be gained by going to
an extreme and suggesting we have come to the conclusion that all men are equal, that there must be no distinction between them. If that were the case it would
have been better had we been numbered instead of named.
If we have been thinking that way we have been thinking
badly.

All men are not equal whether in character, in status, or in
brainpower. Certainly not in brainpower. If the ultra-
socialistic idea—that all men are equal and should therefore
be treated alike—is true, further progress in this world
comes to an end. Progress (in any sense of the word)
means *forward movement*, and if forward movement is to
be made on the assumption that all who move are equal,
the speed of the traffic of human progress must be made
to suit the capabilities of *the slowest vehicle*. And that does
not even bear thinking about.

All men are by no means equal in the sight of man;
neither can it be supposed that men are all equal in the
sight of the Creator of man. Much has been written to the
contrary, but it is not worth reading. The fact remains
that man is judged here largely on his motives, and it is
reasonable to suppose that he is judged wholly on his
motives hereafter. That *must* be, because man's motives,
added up, constitute his life looked at as a whole. No-one
who thinks can ever be persuaded that Adolph Hitler and
St Francis of Assisi have been regarded by Almighty
God with the same feelings. The former was prevented
from subduing whole continents to his evil will, the latter
shed nothing but gentleness round him. God is a God of
love; but it is a mistaken notion to think He regards a
monster of evil as tenderly as He loves an earthly saint.

No; all men are not equal. Because of that it becomes you and me to treat them *as though they were*—for who made any of us judges of men? We are not within our right to make a fellow-creature uncomfortable in our presence. If we do that, there is something definitely wrong with our mental tendencies. We have developed yet another form of the complex inferior. If that is the case, there is no hope of a really tranquil mind.

It is not our attitude towards others when they please or displease us that counts: it is our attitude towards *all* men.

Now it may be that, through almost any cause, you and I can honestly protest that we suffer hardship. We can say with justification that we are being called upon to suffer more than we need. Even so, philosophy teaches that if we allow the *thought* that we are suffering hardship to remain with us, we are simply making that hardship *hardership*. We are adding the thought to the actual condition.

Hardship produces acute worry and distress, and it is difficult to see how a mind so distressed can be expected to know peace. The answer, of course, is that it will *not* know peace. So that it is the actual condition of distress itself which has to be tackled—quite apart from the condition of hardship which causes that distress. The mental act of determination not to worry may do something, but making up one's mind not to worry about worrying matters is really not making up anything very much. Making up one's mind to tackle the cause of the worry, with one's mind perfectly at peace, is what philosophy teaches. Philosophically sound that must surely be, if only because the opposite state of affairs—tackling a problem with a mind disturbed and flustered—generally makes the problem assume larger proportions. A problem tackled in a perfectly calm frame of mind is bound to be reduced; one tackled in a disturbed frame of mind is likely to retain its dimensions at the very least.

And, in tackling a problem, if you or I are quick to take the view that progress *is* being made, if we grasp at any little success we may come by, we shall find a spiritual response and a certain sense of peace will pervade our minds. The mental strength thus obtained acts in reverse: we continue to tackle our problem with increased power.

In other words, we have developed an elementary form of the superiority complex which means that our tendency of mind is humble—but virile. Humility and virility may seem odd companions, but actually they can combine and form a great mental force. Christ was humble, but in his humility lay a good deal of his power. The Son of God never assumed airs and graces; his complexes were so superior that he knew his power and used it perfectly. On one occasion (there may have been others not recorded) he gave strict injunctions to those who witnessed what he did to keep silence about it. We know that they talked all the more, but that makes no difference to Christ's own attitude as we view it now. No-one could have been more virile than God's Son; but no-one could have been more humble than he. He never suffered from the complex inferior; what he had to say he said clearly and definitely, without the least suggestion of either arrogance or affectation.

Christ's mind was always serene. Twice only did he seem seriously disturbed. The first occasion was when his emotions got the better of him and he wept over Jerusalem; the second was when he realized what he was facing that night in the Garden of Gethsemane. Otherwise, whatever difficulties faced him, he tackled them with complete serenity of mind. His philosophy was simple all through. His teaching alone shows that. He taught simple people and clever people alike—always in a simple fashion. And the principles he established—largely because they were so simple—have formed the basis of our best thinking ever since.

So that it is possible to obtain and retain a tranquil mind even while tackling the most worrying problems. It is equally possible to know peace of mind even if we have to live in an environment anything but peaceful.

It largely depends upon what we do with our thoughts when alone. It must depend on that because in moments

I

of solitude we are most vulnerable. Torturing thoughts will come if we let them; but if we deal with them the instant they flash upon our consciousness, we can still retain our serenity. The more we practise, the greater the serenity. *Technique again.*

As a title for a book, *A Tranquil Mind* may appear to suggest something reposeful and even sleepy; but this is a lively world, and you and I are required to live a lively life in it. The only philosophy the Supreme Philosopher approves must be that which teaches us that life on earth is worth taking in full stride. Our environs must be partly responsible for what we are, and for what we make of things here, merely because we are bound to absorb influences. It is for us to use our power to think sufficiently well to absorb what is worth absorbing and to turn down the rest.

Uncongenial surroundings and companions can only disturb our peace of mind in so far as our minds are unresisting. The only type of resistance worth offering is the thinking of peaceful thoughts. That kind of resistance has terrific power; in the midst of strife round us we can be at peace so long as our mental tendencies remain in the category called superior.

For the rest, we can look out of our windows without really seeing what is drab and ugly; we can pass down familiar streets without even being wholly conscious of the depressing effect they so often have had. We can work in the dullest of offices, or the dingiest of factories, and leave them at the end of the day quite unaffected. We can so train our minds that we can take interest, even pride, in the most uncongenial tasks; we can travel in crowded trains and buses and be miles away in thought. It is simply and solely a question of the superiority complex in its most elementary form: we can be *above* everything, anything.

If a tranquil mind is really to be ours—and there is no earthly (and certainly no heavenly) reason why it should not be—we must begin with our environment and environs; we must begin by rising above everything connected with familiar places and familiar people. This does not mean that we should keep aloof from those round us. By that nothing is to be gained and far too much to be lost. But loving thoughts engender loving thoughts, tenderness begets tenderness; if we allow thoughts of an ill nature to leave us, similar thoughts will leave other people. None of which can ever make for our peace of mind. No; our policy must ever be to seek peace and ensue it.

There will be times (as there must have been times in the past) when we shall be moved to speak our real thoughts, especially to those nearest us; but every time we go so far away from what philosophy teaches we endanger our peace of mind. Quarrels have an unpleasant way of coming back upon the quarrellers. Figuratively speaking, it is a case of those using the sword running the risk of perishing by the sword. There is no philosophy that upholds such methods.

On the other hand, there is no call for you or me to stand bad treatment without protest; it is the *nature* of the protest which counts. It is one thing to protest against unfair treatment or to rebuke evil-doing; it is quite another to do either in such a way as to make things worse and to provoke further trouble.

The value of a protest is vested in the effect it produces.

It is, again, one thing to get one's own way when the getting of it is vital; it is quite another to create the impression that there are only two ways, the one that is *not* ours being the wrong one. The result of that kind of attitude comes back upon us all.

Such, then, is the first part of a study of the superiority complex—in other words, of the power to resist the influences of environment by radiation of peaceful thinking. Thoughts are forces, and the forces of peace are always as strong as the forces of strife; often stronger. It is for us to radiate peace in our environed circles.

I now ask you again: Have you ever watched a dancer dancing in a circle of light? If you have, you will remember that wherever he went . . . *the light went also.*

IX

A TRANQUIL MIND IN SPITE OF
CRITICISM

IN the *Oxford Dictionary* the word *criticism* is defined as
'the action of criticizing or passing (especially unfavourable)
judgement upon the qualities of anything; fault-finding.' A
critic is defined as 'one who pronounces judgement on any
thing or person, especially a censurer, a caviller.' The
secondary meaning is given as 'one skilled in literary or
artistic criticism; a professional reviewer; also one skilled
in textual or biblical criticism.'

Now we know where we are—or do we? I am not at all
sure. The Greek word *krites* (pronounced *krit-ees*) means a
judge, a discerner, an arbiter. Those three meanings, to
my way of thinking, exactly define the word *critic*. There
should be no suggestion of anything unfavourable, of
fault-finding, or of cavilling. Such a suggestion gives a bias
to the word; it is a lopsided view of it.

Criticism is judgement, pure and simple. Discernment
pure and simple. Arbitration, pure and simple. If we judge
any thing or anybody, our job is to discern, to look into
thoroughly, to examine accurately.

Having begun by saying all this, may I ask you to bear
with me while I discuss the value of criticism and the
splendid use to which your and my critical faculties can be
put? I feel I must do that before I accept the *Oxford Dictionary's* view of what criticism is. After that, I shall be compelled to accept the word in the sense of fault-finding in
order to deal with the question of *a tranquil mind in spite of
criticism*. Indeed, it will have already occurred to you that
I *have* accepted it by using it in my title.

Are you yourself critical? I personally hope you are
because, if you are not, your mind is in a static condition.
And that, in this advanced twentieth century when everything round you moves quickly, is a weak condition.
We all need our wits about us these days; otherwise our
lives are not safe on the roads. We need to keep alive.

Save.physical incapacity alone, there is no excuse for our remaining only half awake.

But in what sense are you critical? In what degree are you critical? Can you see through a brick wall as quickly as the next man? Are your powers of discernment up to standard? I have no means of knowing what are your answers to these questions, but I can at least present a point of view upon them for your consideration.

A really sound critic is first and foremost appreciative of all that is good, bad, or indifferent, in whomsoever or what-soever he criticizes: *appreciative*. If you come to think of it, that is quite a disarming term. It sounds as though all criticism should be the kind which lets everyone off lightly; but at this point it might be as well to examine the *Oxford Dictionary's* definition of the verb *appreciate*. It is given as 'to form an estimate of worth, quality, or amount; to estim-ate aright; to be sensitive to, or sensible of, any delicate impression or distinction.'

I think that is enough to go upon. Combining the two thoughts, criticism is the act of estimating with absolute accuracy the worth of anybody or any thing. And a very workable definition it is.

The essence of criticism — being precise estimation—is truth. Of that there can be no question; but how far is any of us justified in telling bare and unvarnished truths? In one sense of the expression, to tell the truth is required of us all—but, where others are concerned, are we to tell the truth at all costs, no matter how high those costs may be? By doing that we may cause to arise resentment, anger, shame, bitterness, and other undesirable emotions. The answer must always be that we are justified in telling the truth *in so far* as it does not wound another person.

There are — there certainly are — exceptional instances when the truth has to be told regardless of the consequences; but such cases are better regarded as exceptions to an excellent rule that truth-telling is a very moderate game to play. To tell the truth, by a pronouncement of judgement, is something that must always be done at least with the idea of making the person to whom we tell the truth *feel as we do about it.* If we can do that, we stand a chance of doing something worth while; if we cannot, we have at least partly defeated our own ends.

The same idea has been suggested long ago by the editors in Fleet Street, most of whom hold to the view that news-paper and journalistic criticism should reflect the minds of the readers of the journals. Much the same thing applies in ordinary life. If it happens to be our purpose (for any reason) to criticize another person, and we set about it in such a fashion as to put that person's back up, a good part of the value of our criticism is lost. He whom we criticize may be resentful or roused to anger. The fact that our criticism is justified does not in the least degree alter the situation. The melancholy fact remains that the person we criticize is in no mood to accept even the finest expressions we make use of. After his anger has subsided he may actually see the point of what we have told him; even so, our criticism has been at fault. The next time we have anything to say in judgement upon him we shall have to go warily or we shall do more harm than we did the first time. He will have his weather eye on us for long enough.

If, on the other hand, we have a splendid way of deliver-ing censure, and can leave him thinking well of us and of the help we have given him, we are in a very different case. He will consider us to be really sound; and that, if you come to estimate it, is about the highest compliment he can pay anyone.

If our judgement *is* really sound, that pleasing fact will soon be recognized by those who know us; consequently our advice and counsel will frequently be sought. We shall become known for wisdom, just as was our old friend King Solomon. It is worth it every time, because if our judgement is known and respected for its soundness we have the right to satisfaction on that account. We shall begin to realize that we have absorbed still more of the superiority complex.

We can afford to be humble about it, for all that. It will be a pity if we, on finding our judgement sought because of its excellence, also find our heads being turned a little on account of that discovery. If that happens, it must only mean that we have absorbed a little of the *in*feriority complex.. In other words, if the superiority complex can be regarded as *red*, a little *pink* has seeped through—*and is showing*. One of the most noticeable forms of the complex inferior is when it causes one's head to be turned. Just a little conceit after a success; that is all it amounts to—*but it will show*.

Critical faculties were given to you and to me to use. We are neither of us expected to go through life here without noticing everything that goes on round us. Indeed, we are not doing our job *unless* we notice everything. Unless we do that we are likely to apportion blame, or even praise, inaccurately. The more intensive thinking we do, the more likely are we to sharpen up our critical faculties until they act in 'split seconds'. That is what we all need; but our attitude over the whole business of criticizing requires to be brought under constant review if we are to make a success of it.

The greatest critic imaginable must be the Creator Himself. There can be nothing He does not see—and appreciate at its true worth. A God who is almighty and omnipotent cannot miss very much, one would think; but if He were a God who estimated you and me at our absolute worth, judged us with perfect precision, never allowed us anything unless we completely deserved it, added up the debit side of our account and placed it by the credit side, never let us off until we had paid the uttermost farthing— where should we be? Would our lot be enviable? I do not think mine would be.

Fortunately, God is not like that. He is a God of love. No-one knows quite what it means when we say that God *is* love —but it has a comforting sound about it. At least we know Him to be a God who can be relied upon to be understanding where we are concerned. It comes to much more than that, added up; but it soon resolves into philosophy and means that every time you or I help someone else, every time our judgement is sweetly kind, every time we raise a stumbler to his feet, we become dearer to the hear of the Almighty.

There is another side to this question of the faculty

critical. As I pointed out in the first part of this book, there is a technique to everything affecting us humans. Nothing worth the doing can be done without technique—and no technique can be gained except by study and practice. To which I add here, to conform with my theme of critics and criticism: *no technique can be gained without criticism.*

Doing things well, instead of doing them moderately well, is always worth while; but, in order to do anything well, one must bring one's methods of doing it constantly under review. What is that but criticism? And the greater the critical powers the greater the resultant technique. If we teach others, the same thing applies: the more perfect our criticisms are, the greater the result in our pupils.

If you think of your earlier days when you were at school, you will remember your masters or mistresses and their methods of teaching. They all found fault and made corrections; but some sent you away feeling that you were improving, and that there was some hope of your eventually doing well. Others sent you away quite certain you were no good, and never would be any good. You knew, long before you left that school, who could teach and who could not. You knew where you could go for help and where you could not. You were wise in your generation; there were 'no flies on you' in that respect.

There certainly is a way to teach, and a way not to teach. If you yourself teach, your complex must be superior. Then, for God's sake, make your pupil's complex superior! If you ask him a question and find he is distressed because he does not know the answer, *tell* him the answer! Remind him later of both the question and the answer you gave; then drive the impression straight into his brain by asking the question a third time, if necessary. Then, in nine cases out of every ten, you will *get* the answer. And if you do get the answer you have the satisfaction of knowing you have taught him something; he will go away with the same satisfaction: he will realize he has learnt something. Treat him as you would have him treat you. Hold him in such respect as you would have him pay to you. Send him away feeling, as we say so vividly, 'on top of the world'.

That is the true critical attitude. When we give information we should contrive to give it in such a way that the person who asked for it does not think we consider him a fool for *having* asked for it; if we do that we do something for his tendency of mind. In other words, we help to make *his* complex superior. More important still, we do something for the tranquillity of his mind.

The converse is certainly true; for if we send him away feeling discouraged, indignant, or even defiant, we have definitely disturbed his peace of mind. Does it lie within our right to disturb anyone else's peace of mind by our attitude towards him? We, who seek a tranquil mind because there is nothing in the world we can need more, can hardly expect to attain it while we disturb the tranquillity of other people's minds.

The thought has brought me back to the title of this chapter: *a tranquil mind in spite of criticism.*

From this point onwards, criticism must definitely be taken to be of the negative kind: fault-finding, cavilling, carping. We are all guilty of it at times. It is hard not to be because it is so easy to say that something is wrong and forget what to say to put it right. We are all guilty of it and, conversely, we all suffer from it. Which means that our own tranquillity is disturbed by it.

Of course, we can take what seems to be the line of least resistance: we can ignore it and proceed despite it. But is that really the line of *least* resistance? I think not. If we have to force ourselves to ignore what we should very much like to reply to, our attitude must be so stiff that we are actually taking the line of most, not least, resistance. We shall have to offer more and more vigorous resistance—and there will be precious little tranquillity during a process of that sort.

Then what are we to do? Are we to listen to everyone else's opinion and have none of our own? Are we to take to heart everything people say to us, or about us? Are we to go so far as to *invite* criticism by adopting the pose that we are very humble-minded, that we make a habit of asking people's opinion before proceeding on any course? The answer must be in the negative on all counts.

To begin with, it is impossible to please everybody or
even half everybody. If you do not believe that, ring up the
programme-planners at Broadcasting House. They will
enlighten you.

The only way to tackle this question of criticism by other
people is to subdivide the people. There must be those who
have a right to criticize; there must be those who have no
such right; and there must be the general public who *always*
criticize.

If we undertake any responsibility *we are responsible to
someone* for what we undertake. That person has a right to
criticize. Whether we are paid for what we undertake, or
not, does not greatly signify except that, if we *are* paid, it
is a case of employment. That, naturally, strengthens the
position of the employer who certainly has a right to
criticize.

The question is: how are we going to take an employer's
criticism? It is not a question of whether the criticism is
deserved or undeserved; it is a question of how we, personally, are going to take such criticism, and of how far we are
going to allow it to affect our tranquillity. What is our
attitude to be?

Basically, the reply must be that it is one's duty to note
such criticism and, if possible, to benefit by it; certainly to
abide by it. Where philosophy comes in so neatly is where it
points out that what is worth doing is worth doing perfectly,
if perfection is attainable. That principle has to be followed
out by all of us; otherwise technique remains far from us.
Where the inferiority complex is likely to creep in is where
we mingle our lost patience with a hopeless outlook, or
where it prompts us to brazen everything out by persuading
ourselves we know, when all the time we do *not* know.

The superiority complex is a much more powerful tendency
of mind because it never causes us to lose our balance.
With our tendencies highly superior we tackle our difficulties in a fine spirit and preserve a fine balance. In other words,
we accept criticism graciously and without the least show of
resentment. He who criticizes will not be long in recogniz-
ing our attitude of mind because, if we refuse to take criti-

cism and evince resentment every time it is offered, he who criticizes will soon learn what to expect.

It is when we are alone, and away from the scenes of work, that the memory of mental disturbance (after criticism has been passed) is likely to come back on us. Then our tranquillity is almost sure to be disturbed, and much in the same way as it was during the day. Merely putting the whole thought of it from the mind until we are once more on the scenes of our work does very little. It really contravenes the laws of both philosophy and psychology, and is not worth trying to any extent.

In the psychological sense, there is an excellent method of tackling such a question as this. By devoting a little time each night, just before sleep, to thinking out in (perfect serenity of mind) our approach to our work, we make a very effective and lively experiment in time. If we also rehearse our attitude to our employer, or to whomsoever is our critic, we do much towards finding the best way of treating him. It is the question of a well-ordered mind and its power to deal serenely with what really causes extreme agitation within that mind; but every little success brings relief. Conversely, every little failure adds to the agitation; but nothing is to be gained by an attempt to dismiss the whole thing: *it must be dealt with*. Technique matters in this because it *always* matters. If we can acquire such technique that our attitude is impeccable, the very knowledge that it *is* so will bring tranquillity when we are alone and inclined to turn things over. The ultimate state is not ignoring what is palpably too noticeable to ignore, but valuing it precisely at its true worth. To prevent torturing thoughts coming back upon us when we are alone we need a high technique in the art of sending forth powerful, peaceful thoughts when we are *not* alone.

So that if, while we are within range of criticism (from someone who has the right to criticize) we contrive to keep a perfect balance of mind when actually under its fire, when at last we are alone at night torturing thoughts are less likely to come. In course of time they will *never* come, and our tranquillity will not be disturbed on this account.

Then there is the question of dealing with criticisms from those who have no right to criticize but probably think they have. We find many of these among our relatives, even our best friends. They are in a different class altogether from those who have the right to criticize. Consequently, much of their criticism can run off our backs as water does off a duck's, but (to change the metaphor) if enough mud is slung some of it may stick.

In dealing with such criticism, each of us does a wise thing if we indulge in a little *self*-criticism. Circumstances vary; but if we seem to come in for more criticism and fault-finding than we can reasonably consider we deserve, we can do worse than seek for the cause of it at short range and find out whether or not we *attract* it.

In our schooldays we all knew the type of boy or girl who generally managed to be thrown into the deep end of the swimming bath; or the type of child who stood up to construe a French sentence and then sat down on a bent pin kindly placed on the seat by a loving schoolmate. On the other hand, we also met the opposite type of youngster to whom nothing of the kind ever happened. We can recall a number of children who commanded something very like respect from the rest of the school; we remember that the Head made prefects out of some of them.

We met a few bullies, too. We also met many who were bullied, but more still who were not. It was rarely a question of physical strength preventing their being bullied: it was purely a question of their attitude of mind. Such children began early in their careers to develop at least the beginnings of the superiority complex with the happy result that no-one ever laid a finger on them. There was something about them that caused a bully to halt before he bullied.

What was true of them *then* is true of grown men and women *now*. Some attract criticism—and get it; others seem naturally to repel it. We are all acquainted with personalities whom everyone seems to criticize; we know others we never hear a word against. From the former no-one will hear *one word* of criticism; to the latter most people seem to look up and almost *ask* for their criticism. Their strength of character, united to their unalterable sweetness of disposition, disarms anyone bold enough to criticize them.

Theirs is a simple philosophy. They leave their homes in the morning and leave peace behind them; they return in the evening and bring still more peace with them. Such as they have tranquillity merely because their minds know a serenity that can only come from the Serene Himself.

Their position (in the society they move in) is assured because nothing of the inferiority complex lingers about them; thus they are never guilty of imagining they are 'somebody', as we say. Instead, they are *who* they are, and everyone knows *what* they are.

So that, if you and I find we are coming in for what we consider an undeserved amount of criticism, we do well to take a short-range view of ourselves. Having done that, we can take a fairly long-range view of other people. Naturally there will be a few impossibles among them—the kind we dislike at heart but have, for some reason or other, to put up with. The kind whose tongues hang in the middle, in whose keeping no-one's character is safe. They are to be found everywhere, and we all suffer from them. If ours is the complex superior we can usually deal with them successfully. We can even make them eat their words without offering such words on a plate. We can disarm them by our own splendid poise.

Should we really dislike them, *we do them a bad turn* if we allow distasteful thoughts to remain with us where they are concerned. If we do that, we are also weakening our *own* defences against them because we are allowing *our memories of them* to disturb our peace of mind.

The line of least resistance here is *not to allow their images* to remain in our minds for more than a few seconds at a time. We can adopt the attitude that it is time enough to think about them when we are actually face to face with them; after they have gone, whatever they have done and however objectionable they may have been, we can afford to dismiss them from our mental vision.

It is the same if we have had the misfortune to quarrel with someone to such an extent that we cannot even meet that person. That sometimes happens; it has to be dealt with properly if our peace of mind is not to be disturbed on account of it. Philosophically, it is our *duty* not to let that person's image remain within our mental vision (which is part of the memory) more than a few seconds at a time, unless circumstance actually compels us to do so.

This brings up the question of a tranquil mind with some force. The mind is so constructed that mental pictures, which are part of the memory, can be brought back at will. I suggest that you yourself can recall every little detail in your own bedroom. You can picture many rooms, equally in detail. You can, for example, reproduce quite a respectable picture of the church you are in the habit of attending, but the detail is not so elaborate. If you have been in a room once only, you cannot expect to be able to picture it in anything like *close* detail.

Again, you can always spend time in reproducing pictures of places where you have been, especially when such places have attracted you. A line of coast—perhaps in Wales—where you once spent a holiday. In a flash you can conjure up a view of some spot you loved in Devon or Cornwall—but, in so doing, you never get *two* pictures to look at *together*. You can never reproduce two photographs on the same film, even though you may have accidentally done that with your own camera. In order to get a new picture its predecessor has to leave your mental vision.

So it is with pictures of people complete with sound-tracks of their voices, their style of conversation, their movements; even their attitude towards yourself. If the mood takes you, it is easily possible to reproduce quite an accurate film-show.

But what if your mood *forces* you to reproduce pictures to look at in this way? What if they *persist* in coming within your vision? What if they come with a noisy sound-track that blares and blasts, almost deafening you with their unjust, unpleasant criticisms? Where does your peace of mind get to when that happens?

There is an answer in philosophy—indeed, there is one in physiology: your film-producing faculties are at your command if your complex is sufficiently superior to *keep* them at your command. If your mind is so constructed that you can have your pictures of Wales, and (when you are tired of them) change over for some more of Devon or Cornwall, you can use the same machinery to change a film that is causing you distress for one that will *not* cause you distress. Practice is necessary—but, then, can you name anything that does *not* improve with practice?

You may complain that you are hyper-sensitive, that you suffer more than other people seem to suffer. The answer in philosophy is: if you are hyper-sensitive you are fortunate because you must have very great powers to enjoy—even if you have often to suffer. That certainly is the value of being hyper-sensitive: one enjoys deeply; one appreciates aesthetic beauty. One certainly suffers, but only in so far as one is able to manage one's complexes.

Hyper-sensitiveness which causes any of us to take offence, should someone offer a word of criticism, is actually a form of the inferiority complex. If we take offence at the slightest provocation we must have adopted the attitude that no-one must say a word to us. That amounts to a false idea of our own personal dignity. It is actually one of the worst forms of the complex inferior.

On the other hand, should we be so thick-skinned that nothing anyone says can have the least effect on us, our sense of values is indeed odd. We may be happy enough in that our minds are possibly at peace, but we shall be missing things we should not miss. A hyper-sensitive nature is often responsible for one's mind being disturbed too easily; but, with one's complex completely superior, even the most sensitive nature can be subdued to circumstance; on the other hand, if one's complex is tainted with inferiority one can suffer acutely.

That is why the superior complex, well developed, is so essential when we come to take a definite course in the face of criticism. Many a man's nerve has been strained when he has gone on in spite of adverse opinion. It may be our lot to have to do that. We may know (not merely *think* we know) that a certain course is right, but find the opposition to it almost unnerving. Yet, if we know we are right, we go on. Ours is the responsibility. If we succeed, ours is the credit; if we fail, ours the shame.

It is then that anyone possessed of a highly-developed superiority complex, realizing he is alone and that his friends oppose him, becomes conscious of his Creator whose criticism is always sound and who becomes conscious of an earth-soul faced with great odds; *the next second* power is flashed across the ether, and the earth-soul's mind is made up: *he goes on*. Great decisions are often made that way. It *is* possible to proceed in spite of the strongest criticism—and without endangering one's peace of mind.

And finally—at least, on this part of my theme—there is the criticism all of us must surely face if we do anything in public. An answer might be that if we do anything in public we must *expect* criticism, that we shall get it whether we expect it or not—but such an answer is not very helpful. All the same, it is unhappily true that if we do anything in public we shall soon find ourselves sorting out our bouquets and keeping them separate from our brickbats. Attitude of mind goes a long way, but it alone will not do everything. Personality—the result of attitude of mind—means much to all who appear in public because the public is quick to value a personality of worth; but even personality does not do everything. You yourself may be the possessor of a charming personality, but charm will not cause you to play the Beethoven violin concerto in public if you are a bad violinist. Only sound technique and advanced artistic perceptions will do that for you.

While our society remains as it is—and as it has been for centuries—there will always be criticism of those whose technique is sound by those whose technique is the reverse of sound. One of the most difficult things professionals have to cope with is unsound criticism by amateurs. It is so easy to become impatient and declare all amateur criticism to be worthless. Most of it is, admittedly; but as amateur critics infest all society, and as they insist on giving their criticisms whether they are wanted or not, their criticism remains part of the burden professionals have to carry.

It is best recognized as such and dealt with carefully. It is so easy to criticize people who appear before the public eye; thus it remains a fact that if you or I do anything in a public capacity we stand to be shot at. It is pointless to make a list of the professions—music, literature, art, the Church, parliament—and take them one by one; professional men and women in *every* walk of life come (almost automatically) under the fire of criticism.

No-one, however good his technique may be, however really great he may be, is actually above criticism; but he is a poor philosopher if he allows criticism to disturb his peace of mind. If he is the possessor of great technique, his complex should be correspondingly superior; consequently his great knowledge should make him humble and powerful at the same time. Our great men and women are the greatest servants the public has. Usually the fact is recognized, even though it is also true that the public never stops to think its criticism may wound a sensitive nature.

Some years ago, I happened to be present at a recital by a young girl whose name was new to me. She was a singer. It was obvious to me that she had appeared in public a little too soon for safety; quite obviously she needed more lessons. What appealed to me about her singing was its freshness, and her voice was in a degree beautiful. On the other hand, her pronunciation of French and German in her lieder-singing was not without fault.

As a musician, I noted her weaknesses immediately; but I thought I detected much promise in that attractive young singer. Unfortunately for her, a well-known music critic was present. I regretted the fact as soon as I saw him, which was after her first group of songs. I thought I could guess what he would write; but I was mistaken. I thought he would at least see the promise of things-to-come in her even though I feared he might be down upon some of her faults.

His criticism was actually an attempt upon his part to be satirical at that young girl's expense. There was no critical, much less musical, value in a line he wrote about her or her concert. What he said was true; but the way in which he said it—his facetiousness, his utter disregard of her feelings,

K

had only one result where she was concerned. I heard privately from one of her friends that she was so deeply discouraged, so intimidated, that she gave up all hope of success. I never saw her name in public again.

The critic's point of view was that he was there to protect the public from buying tickets for poor performances. The man himself actually knew very little about music, and could not have performed in public had his chance of heaven depended on it. He was merely a writer—a journalist with a certain following. His complex was always the same: thoroughly inferior. In this instance— and in many others—he was directly responsible for disturbing the peace of mind of young aspirants to fame, excepting those who managed to get into his good books from the start. In the profession he was mainly held in contempt.

That, to my mind, is a sad story because that particular critic might have been a judge and not a mere caviller. He might have encouraged where he condemned; he might have pointed to weaknesses in such a way as to urge these young people on to success. What an opportunity lost! Even when people *do* try to do things they had better leave alone, nothing is to be gained by breaking their hearts.

'Judge not that ye be not judged', said the Son of the Supreme Judge. What can you and I make of that trite injunction? It is not difficult to read between each word, knowing who it was who said it. And in so doing we can extend it into a beautiful piece of sound and simple philo- sophy: 'When you judge, see that you judge with a sweet mind and a generous heart. Then, because of the sweetness of your judgement, your own peace of mind will never be disturbed by the bitterness of other men's judgements.'

If you and I can do that, when we face Divine judgement after we have finished here and begun there, we shall be unafraid to paraphrase the Psalmist and say, humbly and proudly: '*Please* enter into judgement with Thy servant, O Lord: he has no fear that, in Thy sight, he shall *not* be justified.' But, if it is to be like *that* with us, we must have made a deep study of the superiority complex.

X

A TRANQUIL MIND IN SPITE OF ILL-HEALTH

IT is hard to see how anyone's mind can be wholly at peace unless that person's health is reasonably good; but it is equally hard to see how impaired health can be greatly improved unless the mind is at peace. It seems to work both ways.

It is beyond my powers to make a list of maladies and diseases (temporary or permanent) and to submit a psychological or philosophical method of effecting a cure for them; but I can take a philosophical view of ill-health and the effect it produces on the mind. That it will have to be general is obvious; an extreme view is likely to get us nowhere.

In our time most of us have known what it is to be ill, if only temporarily or spasmodically. Short illnesses, though a nuisance, can hardly be said to cause great disturbance of mind; lengthy or serious illnesses are another matter. To be put out of action for a considerable period—at least to a person whose heart is in his life-work —is no pleasing experience. Such an experience often causes grave anxiety.

First in importance upon the patient himself. The nature of the trouble cannot signify here; it is the fact that one is laid aside which matters. To be in full swing of activity is something no-one can afford to be ungrateful for; to rise in the morning and stretch one's limbs without feeling the slightest twinge of discomfort—let alone pain—should wring an expression of gratitude from the heart.

If pathological knowledge were *common* knowledge, Christian Science would be the safest science in the world; but how few of us know anything about our bodies! Nor is our ignorance surprising when we consider the training undertaken by men who qualify as doctors. If we all possessed their medical knowledge we might all be the physicians who could cure ourselves. We should soon train our minds to make our bodies behave. We should know exactly how to think and how to employ exactly the right thoughts. The trouble is that we are not certain of knowing what thoughts to employ.

The power of the mind over the body is terrific. No-one who has really learnt how to use his power to think will be in two minds about that; but if our own pathological knowledge is deficient, or unsound, it is difficult to see how we are going to set about effecting a cure for anything worse than a headache.

I have already told the story of how a distant relative of mine refused an operation and died from cancer as a result of the refusal. I observe here that, long before *any* situation gets acute enough to warrant an operation, much damage can be done to the body through trying to put right something one does not understand—merely by the exercise of thought. Or even of prayer.

In my view, it is doubtful whether the Great Physician expects any of us to pray in such terms in such circumstances. If, on feeling the result of some symptomatic condition, we pray for a cure *in as many words* it is doubtful whether we are tackling the problem the right way at all. In praying for a cure of something we are suffering from, we are virtually asking for a minor miracle. Hundreds of minor miracles are worked each hour of the day, whether petitioned for or not; but to suggest that, *as a principle*, one should ask for something of the kind I cannot bring myself to do.

It is a sensible thing to pray for good health. Any wise man or woman, whose faith is strong, will do that with conviction. All of us are within our right to attract the attention of the Source-of-power for power to keep fit and well so that our best purposes in life shall not be seriously interfered with; but there are people—you may have met some—who take the view that all one has to do is to ask for the trouble to subside and then to go on as though the trouble were not there, or had never been there. Such faith is definitely to anyone's credit; I should be the last to say otherwise, but whether it is faith altogether well directed I am doubtful.

Philosophy teaches me that such a course means I am not working in harmony with the laws made by the Creator. I am virtually expecting Him to hold a special surgery and to hand me a bottle of what might loosely be called 'spiritual medicine' which, if I take in the doses prescribed, will put me right in no time. Many people whose faith is immense will do that kind of thing and then wonder why they still remain indisposed. If they are tackled on the matter they will usually say that it is God's will that they shall be ill until, in His own good time, they shall be allowed to get well again. Such a theory is hardly worth the holding.

We all do a much more sensible thing if, when we feel there is something wrong, we consult our own doctor. Otherwise, why were doctors ever born, or made? Surely not for members of the community who have no faith in a Supreme Healer?

When we think of all that God has allowed—by sheer use of His own laws—does it not strike us that He has been very good to man? The amazing things that have been done—during the war and since—are quite enough to make us appreciate the progress which has been made since the days when men went to their local apothecary or barber-surgeon to have their blood let.

In these days treatment can be had for the asking. Diseases regarded hitherto as hopeless have been conquered by men who have strained to the utmost the powers their Creator has given them. To seek their advice and obey their injunctions is the act of a sane person; to determine to be one's own physician—however strong one's faith in God may be—is merely subjecting faith to perversion. These men give their whole attention to the exercise of their profession. They concentrate on what is their life-work—the relief of pain and suffering. It is the same with the nurses, many of whom would appear to be angels in a very thin disguise.

Quite obviously the Supreme Physician sent such men, and women into the world for this purpose and this alone. Among them are good, bad, and just moderate technicians; but that is common to all the professions. The fact remains that they are here for a purpose. Where the wisdom of your and my use of our powers of thinking comes in is where we consult our physicians with a *consciousness of God's power to heal while we do it.*

If we persist in leaving our doctor out of the question, and use our power to think solely because we feel justified in asking to be made well, we are going the wrong way about it. We may plead that our duties are important, that we wish to carry them out as perfectly as we are able; we may plead that we have others dependent on us; we may plead that we are trying to be unselfish. All this is grand in its way; but we are *still* going about it wrongly. We are *still* going against the laws God made. We are asking Him to give *us* the answer. We do better when we consider how man's brain is constructed, and that technique is technique in everything affecting us. It is a very simple philosophy indeed which makes us appreciate that an answer from the Supreme Mind will flash a thousand times more effectively *into a doctor's mind* than into our own.

Philosophy insists that, as the laws of nature are what they are, every time you or I contravene them we come down.

Now as to the question of a tranquil mind in regard to all this. You are ill, let us suppose. You have seen your doctor and have been told that you must remain in bed for a time; your appointments must be postponed. All of which has happened at a particularly bad time; in consequence your mind is not at peace.

As a tranquil mind is not likely to be yours just now, philosophy teaches you that you must begin to seek it. Your first chain of thoughts might well be directed against the illness itself; just a calm concentration on your actual suffering. That you bear it without complaint is philosophically sound because the opposite state of mind—being what is so aptly called 'crabby'—is itself a disturbed state of mind. Moreover, if your faith in your Creator is what you have thought it to be, you can occupy yourself with much calm and powerful thinking; but unless such thinking *is* calm it will not be very powerful. You cannot banish your illness any more than you can sleep off insomnia, but you can do much to shorten your illness by *thinking health* into your body. The more you practise such thinking the more powerful your mind becomes. And so you help your physician by getting help from . . . your *Physician*. That *is* scientific, and by no means unchristian.

Your tranquillity may be gravely endangered when someone else in your home is ill; but if you are to retain peace of mind (which you should do for your patient's sake) you must do something definite. You have to remember that the patient's own mind may be anything but at peace. He may not be doing very much towards helping his physician by getting help from the Physician. It is obviously your job to direct every ounce of power you possess towards him. He need not know — indeed, it may be better he does not know—but, all the same, *that is your job*. If you want help for it, you know how it can be obtained. If you are conscious of the Physician, He is conscious of you—and of your patient. Very simple philosophy, that; *but very powerful*.

Such philosophy comes almost naturally into exercise where a sick child is concerned. A baby, especially. We all know mothers who have suffered agonies of mind on account of an ill baby. And yet — one of God's greatest gifts to womankind is the mother's instinct. A mother who can keep her mind steady in an emergency, who can detect the least sign of trouble where her baby's health is concerned, is making direct use of a gift she was given when her baby was born on earth. Nothing is more certain than the mother's instinct. The mother who keeps her mind in a state of calm and tranquillity can do much; it is one of God's own laws that she should.

Lastly, there is the situation caused by conditions that may be alleviated but not actually cured. The thought of anything permanent in the way of bodily affection is horrifying to anyone in good health. Who of us, during the years of war, did not pray that (if we *had* to go) we might be taken direct? Anything rather than be maimed or permanently disabled. Such a petition seemed reasonable enough—at least, most of us thought so at the time. And yet, those who have been so disabled have (it would seem) been in some degree compensated just as those born deaf or blind are compensated.

To our way of thinking, the horror of permanent disablement is thereby lessened in no degree whatever; but the fact remains that those who have suffered so acutely have learned what a tranquil mind is. Cases must differ vastly; but the whole position, viewed broadly, does point to something of the kind having happened.

From such a thought you and I can afford to take heart. We can rise in the morning in thankfulness that another day is beginning and that we have the strength to live it out; we can lie down once more at night in gratitude for our day and with hope high in our hearts that another splendid day will follow. But if we forget to prime our minds, if we omit to do a little forceful thinking, we shall surely find there is something missing. We may find that those tiny torturing thoughts persist in making their presence known. If that happens, we are being called upon to make another effort towards obtaining peace of mind by deliberately preparing our minds to receive it.

How these small things of life matter! How many were the years we let go by before we realized it! And how often are we slow to find out that our habits of life have not helped us to keep in good health!

It is all part of good philosophy—and certainly of the superiority complex—to measure our strength accurately. We all become tired, often when we have spent our best hours doing things for others. Even Christ himself was weary at times—and from the same cause. Yet he went on, taking what rest he could *when* he could.

Christ always knew what to do. He used his mental transmitter and flashed the ether for power to carry on, and the answer came back by natural laws. It is the same for us. We can always get the power to go on because the going-on is most of the reason why we were sent here. None of us leaves life before our time, and no amount of experimenting in time will mean that we shall find out when that is likely to be. That is not our business.

To prime our minds against illness is a sane act; to avoid a mode of life likely to lay us open to illness is equally sane; to remain tranquil during illness seems to be something we owe to ourselves, to say nothing of those about us. The greater issue of life and death is not our affair. We stay here until we are sent for.

Because ill-health (from one cause or another) is so prevalent among us, it has (so to speak) become idiomatic for us to inquire about one another's health when we meet. In one way, it is a pity we do so; but it is so customary that no philosopher will go so far as to suggest a discontinuance of the habit. Chiefly, perhaps, because people are so quick to regard an omission on our part—should we *not* ask them how they are when we meet them—as selfishness. Yet, in some instances, we avoid such inquiry to avoid a tale of woe. To be an interesting invalid seems the greatest aim in some people's lives; it is a positive cult. And there is always *something* the matter with them! The matter, really, is with their minds. A tranquil mind is not theirs because they have not progressed far enough in philosophy to obtain it. People who are always thinking of their ailments rarely think objectively.

I once heard quite a neat reply to a question regarding health. It came from a friend who was asked what had been the matter with him. He shook his head.

'Haven't the least idea', he said. 'On Saturday I thought I should have died; on Sunday *I wished I had*; but I was back in the office as usual on Monday.'

There is something to be said against talking about being ill. If it were the custom of English people to talk about their ailments to the only persons qualified to listen —their doctors—the nation's health might be a shade better. Talking about symptomatic conditions does nothing to prevent their development, and much to weaken resistance against them.

The thought reminds me of an extremely amusing comedian whom I knew intimately years ago. He was causing roars of laughter by trying to teach an audience to sing a ridiculous song. I happened to whisper something to a friend sitting next to me. He noticed my action. Then he sent the audience into a shout of mirth by saying: 'If the gentleman sitting in the front would stop telling the lady next him *all about his operation* he could attend and learn this song.'

There is something deeply philosophical in what was only intended to amuse. We all talk too much about our health. If we said less about our health and more about what we really enjoy, we might enjoy better health. That is a very simple philosophy. If, instead of disturbing our peace of mind still further by giving away the fact that it is *already* disturbed, we developed a thoroughly superior complex and made light of everything (except what is palpably too heavy to be made light of) we should be doing something for ourselves in the first place, and for those nearest us in the second.

Yet, on the other hand, to withhold sympathy from someone who appears (as we say) to be 'under the weather' is an act no philosopher would approve. It is the purest philosophy to suggest that sympathy is something we can always offer but never beg for. Even so, there are times when an omission of reference to health, where a friend is concerned, is good policy. It largely depends on the friend. It is quite easy to say the wrong thing to a neurotic person. One has to be quick to decide how to proceed when one comes across a friend with his tail down. One hardly improves matters by causing him to tuck it right between his legs.

To have brilliant health is a wonderful experience— so wonderful that any of us may fall into a trap where others, whose health is not so good, are concerned. We have to remember that people in ill-health are apt to feel that a really healthy person sucks all the air out of the room. A person in considerable pain can hardly bear the presence of someone who is obviously bursting with good health. Moreover, healthy people sometimes sap the vitality of those less healthy.

The whole question of a tranquil mind in spite of ill-health does revolve round the superiority of one's complex; there is no philosophy that can teach anything to the contrary.

'Good or bad health', wrote Chaulieu, 'makes our philosophy.' That is not true—at least, not in that form. It is nearer the truth to say that our philosophy goes a long way towards making, or marring, our health.

Juvenal said: 'A sound mind in a sound body is a thing to pray for.' It certainly is; and Martial was not far wrong when he said: 'Life is not to be alive, but to be well.'

'Give me health and a day', wrote Emerson, 'and I will make the pomp of emperors ridiculous.' Emerson also said: 'I honour health as the first muse, and sleep as the condition of health.'

And Isaac Walton: 'Look to your health; and if you have it, praise God and value it next to a good conscience; for health is the second blessing that we mortals are capable of—a blessing that money cannot buy.'

To all of which, the simple philosopher adds: 'Keep your mind calm and forceful, that you may the better enjoy good health when it is yours to enjoy, that you may suffer less when it is denied you.'

No philosopher will tell you that to fear illness is to invite it, but most doctors will tell you that your resistance to it lies at least partly in your own hands.

A tranquil mind can be enjoyed in spite of ill-health so long as your complex is not inferior. It is attitude of mind which counts all through—the quiet, powerful thinking that alone is born of consciousness of the Creator's power. It hardly does to carry out the principles of Robert Owen's satirical epigram:

> God and the Doctor alike we adore,
> But only in danger, not before.
> The danger o'er, both are requited:
> God is forgotten, the Doctor slighted.

The simple philosopher, however, finds himself going back to Emerson—even if he takes the liberty of para-

phrasing him, turning what seems a boast into a petition:
'Give me health and a day. Give me health *all* that day. I
will then make any pomp *I* ever had look *utterly* ridiculous.'

Or, more simply still:

'That I may serve a purpose, give me health . . . and
many days!'

XI

A TRANQUIL MIND IN SPITE OF DISAPPOINTMENT

MY first disappointment— at least, the first I can still
remember—came to me on the twentieth day of June in
the year 1897. I was rising eleven. In those days I was
living in Birmingham, and had been taken to see the
procession which celebrated the Diamond Jubilee of
Queen Victoria.

I had looked forward to it for weeks. I had already
examined literally dozens of photographs of the Queen.
As no two were alike, I had concluded that all could not
be good; but that did not greatly trouble me. All that
mattered was: my parents had been invited to join various
other relatives and friends and watch the procession from
an office window in New Street. I remember my pride
because of a new suit I was wearing.

It must have taken well over half-an-hour for the
principal procession to pass by. When it had gone I
dissolved into tears, but nobody seemed to understand why.

I did. I sobbed bitterly. My sobs had the unpleasant
effect of making me wholly inarticulate, but at last I
managed to stammer out the cause of my suffering: *the
Queen was not in the procession.*

To me it was very much like a Punch-and-Judy show
without Punch or, to be more anthropologically correct,
without Judy. Everyone seemed highly amused, and it
was my turn not to understand why. The explanation
given me was that the Queen was in a procession in
London; but no-one could persuade me that London was

IN SPITE OF DISAPPOINTMENT   157

as important as Birmingham, and I refused to be comforted. Then I was given something to eat I had never seen before. They told me it was called *ice-cream*. At first I refused to have anything to do with it. In defence of my attitude I howled all the louder because I had so wanted 'to see the Queen in her crown'. Then someone said she would not be wearing a crown; more likely it would be a bonnet.

At that point, somewhat mollified, I tackled the ice-cream. Now I come to think of it, that ice was merely frozen custard. I distinctly remember the big strawberry which decorated the top of it. Because of that ice I think I was nearer heaven then than I have ever been since. I know my ultimate verdict was that ices were 'better than Queens any day.'

In our childhood's days disappointments were sharply-cut, crystal-clear experiences. And when the grown-ups said 'Don't cry; eat your cake', not all of us were ready to comply. Often it depended upon the quality of the cake more than on the reason for the tears; but in those days we depended so much on the ability of older people to comfort us that disappointments seemed almost to be their affairs rather than our own.

It is an unsatisfactory philosophy—if, indeed, it can be called philosophy—that suggests disappointments are good for us, or that they have a chastening effect upon us. That point of view has been expressed by many people of the old-fashioned type; but it is doubtful whether it has ever done much more than irritate those to whom it has been stated. In the broad sense it may be true that disappointments are not altogether bad for some of us merely because the opposite condition of affairs—success all along the line—may have an unbalancing effect upon the minds of all but the strongest. It may even be true that disappointment and failure have been known to sweeten men's characters and make of them something they otherwise might never have been; but the unqualified statement that disappointment is good for us is not true.

Disappointment is something unpleasant. Disappoint ment which hangs like a cloud over a person's life *for an extended period* generally has an embittering effect upon that person.

If philosophy is to be of the slightest good, it can only be when it teaches us that it is best to begin by accepting facts as they are. Moreover, in order to deal effectively with something we should prefer to avoid if we could, it is as well to make a nice distinction between *disappointments* and *disappointment*.

The plural form suggests individual experiences, presumably of varying intensity; the singular form suggests something worse—a life lived under an ever-deepening cloud. It is one thing to have to face disappointments; it is quite another to have to face—disappointment.

What the plural form suggests is better tackled first—but hardly by adopting as a method the facetious pseudo-proverb: 'Blessed is he who expecteth nothing for he shall not be disappointed when he receiveth it not.' The statement, of course, is just silly, and was probably never intended to be anything else; but it is quotable here because of the germ of truth underlying what might be called the 'expecting part' of it.

There is a fatalistic touch about expecting nothing for fear of disappointment if one expects anything. Such an attitude throws the word *hope* clean out of the dictionary. There is no attitude of mind that can or will prevent disappointment, and there is no philosophy that can suggest such an attitude. Even when there is disappointment over something we have tried to do and have failed at, no attitude of mind could have prevented that failure. That, at least, will do for a general statement. No doubt there are individual cases where the right attitude of mind *could* have done something to prevent the disappointment; but there is no philosophy that can teach you that, even if your mind is rightly set and balanced, you will *never* suffer disappointment. It cannot be otherwise because so many disappointments come from a set of circumstances completely out of one's control.

So that we are forced to accept what is a very elementary fact: disappointments will come, failures will occur, and accidents will happen, whether we add the bit about the 'best-regulated families' or not. To that part of it philosophy has not a word to say. It is only with regard *to our attitude in taking* the disappointment that philosophy can be of use. In that it can help a good deal; so can the superiority complex.

Disappointments can easily be divided into those affecting ourselves—our own personal disappointments— and those we suffer because other people are not what we expected they would be, or because they have let us down in some other way.

Our own first. Conveniently subdivided thus: disappointments caused by our not *getting* what we want, not *doing* what we want, not *being* what we want. Most personal disappointments fall naturally under one of these three headings. May I here repeat that these are disappointments—plural—and therefore separate experiences; also that it is entirely a question of our taking such disappointments in a way that prevents their disturbing our tranquillity. There is no question of their being *prevented*.

Not getting what we want is often bitterly disappointing. We have all met people who tell us they can always do without what they cannot get. We cannot be too sure of these people—or, at least, of their statements. Usually, when people talk like that, we can safely conclude: either they have suffered so much from disappointments that they have adopted an attitude for show purposes, or that their complexes are *really* superior. It is doubtful whether the latter is the case because, if it were, we should hear nothing about it. We should, on the contrary, be admiring them for the fineness of their bearing; we should appreciate that, whatever they have suffered, they are proceeding on their way with a show of splendid strength. If they act for show purposes, it is far more likely that they have developed yet another form of the inferiority complex—one responsible for their attempt to create an impression. The impression they wish to give is that, despite all they have suffered, they are still wonderful specimens of humanity. Not a very harmful form of the complex, admittedly; but all forms of that complex have an unpleasant habit of spreading themselves into other, and possibly worse, forms.

The secret of tackling disappointments lies primarily in keeping everything connected with them a dead secret. If we are disappointed because something we wanted is not to be had, we act against the laws of philosophy when we unburden ourselves to someone else. If we do that we merely offer proof that we have caught yet another dose of the poorer complex —because we are showing weakness. It *is* weakness if we cannot keep our own secrets. We are not only admitting that we are suffering from disturbance of mind because we cried for the moon and were not even placated with a star, but we are disturbing someone else's mind by virtually demanding sympathy.

If we are taken into someone else's confidence, and a long tale of misery and vexation is poured into our ears, we like to think we use our utmost power to help that person; but it is not necessarily our privilege to *ask* for sympathy. With a complex highly superior we shall prefer to deal with our own miseries and vexations. There are, naturally, exceptions to what may not really be a rule; but the general attitude engendered by such thinking is correct enough. It is always our good office to give the soundest advice and the kindliest comfort we are capable of; but it is not, philosophically speaking, our province to ask for a like office to be done for us. I feel I must insist on this.

So that the secret of tackling disappointments lies in the secrecy itself. It must be so because the opposite state is philosophically unsound. If we seek solace by unburdening ourselves to others we are fanning the flame of a disappointment by going through its details, whereas philosophy suggests we should stifle the remembrance of it. If we are seeking a tranquil mind in spite of it all, the less we allow the remembrance to remain with us the sooner do we bring about a better state of thinking. Stifling remembrance of disappointments .means that, gradually, they fade from the memory; encouraging the mind to remain conscious of disappointments amounts to *fretting*. We cannot fret and be at peace.

So that, as secrecy is the best policy, it follows that if we receive a shock of disappointment in the presence of someone else, we either turn it off lightly or say nothing; the opposite of that is an upset of balance and poise. Inwardly we may know what it feels like to be stabbed; but if we control our rage, if we refuse to display the least sign of what we really feel, we do something for ourselves in very deed. The *next* disappointment we are called upon to sustain, even though it be greater, even though it has to be added to all previous disappointments—the *next* disappointment leaves us in an altogether stronger position. To argue that we are too sensitive to disguise our feelings under strain is no argument at all. There is an answer in philosophy we cannot pass by: if we are so sensitive that we display exactly what we feel, without restraint, we cause distress to someone else's mind. The more that person loves us the greater the distress.

We have only to reverse the positions to realize this. If we are compelled to witness the tears, the rage, the utter dejection, of someone we love, we are distressed on that person's behalf. We can at least afford to remember that it works both ways, and to appreciate the fact that it is against the laws of philosophy to disturb the peace of mind of another person because of what has happened to ourselves. Only a complex with inferior tendencies can be responsible for what is quite a gross form of selfishness.

The powerful mind, when tortured by disappointment, changes its whole train of thought. The mind is so constructed that when a space occurs, or is made to occur, something has to fill that space. By using our power to think—in other words, by employing the driving power of our souls—it remains for us to fill *all* spaces. If the continuity of our peaceful thinking is disturbed by the incursion of disappointment, and a space occurs merely through the shock of it, it is the powerful mind which accepts the disappointment in complete calm, whatever course is subsequently taken to deal with the details. If the reaction in the mind is such that you or I can fill in all spaces caused by shock of disappointment, we shall make

L

do very well without what we have so wanted but have been denied. That is what is popularly known as 'being philosophical over it'.

That we have a right to get what we want, so long as what we want is right in itself, is unquestionable. If we are disappointed—and yet our complexes are all superior— our very resistance against the effect of the disappointment is enough in itself to raise the power of our minds to a higher level. It *is* a question of doing without what we cannot obtain; but it is also a *condition* of mind that makes for *peace* of mind. None of us can afford to put such a condition away from us; if our complexes are as they should be we shall remain tranquil and totally unaffected by *any* shock of disappointment.

Not being able, or allowed, to *do* what we want is another type of disappointment. Here it is the sense of frustration that rakes our nerves and disturbs our peace. If such frustration follows an attempt to elbow a passage through a crowd of circumstances, we are left to consider whether or not it was a bad thing to be disappointed. Elbowing our way through crowds is bad for their ribs and worse for our elbows. If someone in that crowd of circumstances can (figuratively) point an accusing finger and say something about our always 'wanting our own way', there is something wrong with our complexes. Half the disappointments any of us suffer (because we want to do something and find there are reasons why we may not do it) arise from desires within us that are exceptionable. Even so, there is not much point in dealing with disappointments caused by our prime conceptions being ill-managed except to observe that, if they *are*, there can be no question of a tranquil mind. There is only point in dealing with disappointments of this nature in so far as our reasons for wanting to take a certain course are *un*exceptionable.

If our reasons really are unexceptionable, the very fact that we *know* the best thing we can do is to take a certain course makes the disappointment all the greater when we are frustrated. If our complexes are so superior that we know we cannot possibly have made a mistake, if we can see when others are apparently blind, our sense of frustration can certainly be acute. But that very sense of frustration is what should cause a powerful reaction. While it is always useless to kick against the pricks, a really strong-minded person—as distinct from a pig-headed one—adjusts his mind as he rises against the effects of being forbidden to do, or being prevented from doing, something he knows to be right.

Cases vary so much that it is impossible to give a comprehensive example; but the real philosopher, seeing which way the wind is blowing, sets his philosophical sail accordingly; he never allows the sense of frustration to remain in his mind. He clears it out and fills the space more usefully. Allowing a sense of frustration to remain in the mind means that peace can never enter it.

The third division I have suggested covers a wide field: it is disappointment because we may not *be* what we want. We may want to be clever or we may want to be rich, and see no chance of being either; we may realize that because we are not clever we are never likely to be rich. Here the limits of philosophy are passed because there is no philosophy that can make us either clever or rich; but there is a philosophy that will teach us something better than to cry for the moon.

Apart from the thought of cleverness or wealth, to be what one always wanted to be—and to make a success of being it—is a grand experience. The greater the success the stronger the conviction that one is really doing what one was sent to do. A tranquil mind, in such circumstances, should not be difficult to attain—provided there is nothing else to oppose it. But to have deeply desired to be one thing, and to have been forced by circumstance to be something else, is quite another matter. Yet there is an answer in philosophy for it.

To allow the thought of a major disappointment of that kind to pervade one's thinking is to contravene the laws of philosophy. One's life-work, admittedly, is never then first-grade; it is, at the highest, a kind of 'best seconds'. The original sense of disappointment and frustration has undergone a kind of chemical change: it has dissolved into dissatisfaction. Everything connected with one's work is then tinged with the sense of discontent even though one may be actually brave enough not to show it. When that happens to any of us we may manage to keep the fact from our friends, but even that admirable show of bravery and balance does not reduce the effect upon ourselves. Looking at everything through sun-glasses, even when ophthalmically necessary, means accepting discoloration. Applied to life, such a philosophy makes everything seem slightly under par; the brilliance of even the best of one's attainments suffers an eclipse.

Wishing for something better hour by hour, day by day, and even year by year, means wasting valuable time at a wishing-well, forgetting that the days when fairies did such splendid work for mankind have either passed or never existed. To metamorphose the dissatisfaction into a mere daydream is all very well in its way; any philosopher will back you up if you do it if only because you stand at least some chance of a more peaceful state of mind; but if you do too much of that kind of thing you may find the realities of life, when at last you allow yourself to come back to them, are in themselves disappointing.

The whole point of life on this earth lies in living for what we are, not for what we wish we might have been. However humble our position may be, however unimportant it may seem, philosophy insists that we *must be* what we *are*, that we must carry out our purposes with dignity and distinction. Ambition, rightly thought about and rightly used, is a grand virtue. If we have no ambition we have no spirit; if we have no spirit we have no real incentive to live—and we have to remember that we *must* live until we are sent for. It is for us to see we live (and not merely exist) because this life is a preparation for the next. It is quite possible we may, one day, be asked what we did with our earthly life and how we enjoyed it. It will be a thin answer to give if we are forced to admit we did not really live at all, that we merely dragged our way through an existence we are now thankful is over.

Dissatisfaction is an ugly word—or, at least, it has a grim thought underlying its etymology. *Satis*, enough; *factum* from *facere*, to make; *dis*, the negative: *we did not make enough* of things. That is what dissatisfaction amounts to. These Latin derivatives have a way of telling us the truth sometimes.

And so we come to the thought of *disappointment* in the collective sense of a number of disappointments, to the dreadful thought of what total disappointment can be, in spite of all we may have done to counteract individual disappointments as they appeared one by one. Failure to reach the height we set out to reach; failure to attain the technique we aimed at; failure to develop the power we hoped to develop—especially if we have gripped the fact that we all have to live as members of society and that it is our bounden duty to take our place *in* that society. We find it no small matter—and certainly no pleasing matter —to have to say to ourselves: 'I have just done nothing worth while.' It is no comfort to say: 'Of course, I aimed too high.'

No philosopher will back you, or me, in that way of thought. Where philosophy steps in is where it makes a very simple suggestion: namely, that we begin all over again and first of all count our blessings. If we really have striven and struggled for a position in life we could have been proud of, and yet it has not come our way, we can afford to regard that struggle with honest pride. We can do worse than appreciate that unless we had made that struggle, unless we had striven so earnestly, unless we had taken disappointments time and time again, *we should have done much worse*. We should never have been where we are, even though that may not be anywhere near where we wanted to be.

It is all a question of *being* what we *are*, and of what is our attitude to others who are also being what they are. It is all a question of our being here for a while with a life to live which we shall be accountable for later.

We shall never be asked to account for what we *might* have been, but only for what we actually *have* been. When we come to review our lives here with Him who sent us

here, we shall feel awkward if we have to go over periods
spent at various wishing-wells; they will seem so futile.
How much more satisfactory to Him, and to us, if we and
our Creator can review together a grand period of honest
and dignified progression, of technique splendidly acquired!
It does not strain the imagination to picture the Judge
commenting on such progression and saying: '*You made a
fine thing of this part of your life; you deserved the tranquillity
you experienced*'.

Such tranquillity must have resulted from our possession of a highly superior complex. It can have come no
other way. There could never have been any wearing of
green-tinted glasses (supposing jealousy to be as green as
it has been painted) and no 'complex inferior' to cause us
to envy others who may have climbed somewhere out of
our own personal reach.

I have a word to say about hope at this point, mainly
because most philosophers tread carefully when called upon
to deal with it.

Hope is an oddity in the philosophical sense. Our good
friend St Paul classed it as one of the three heavenly
graces. No doubt it is; but it is odd, for all that. The *Oxford
Dictionary* insists that it is 'expectation of something
desired' or 'desire combined with expectation'.

H'm! I am not so sure about that. Personally, I think
that Locke, in the second volume of his *Human Understanding*, brought off a fairly neat definition of *hope*, even
though he had to use many more words to do it. He says
that 'hope is that pleasure in the mind, which everyone
finds in himself, upon the thought of a profitable future
enjoyment of a thing which is apt to delight him.' Rather
a wordy definition, but it does seem to get near the truth.
I could accept the *Oxford Dictionary's* ideas of what hope
is, if it qualifed 'expectation'. It seems to me that hope is
'*reasonable* expectation of something desired', or 'desire
combined with '*reasonable* expectation.' *Unless* the word
expectation is so qualified it seems to me that the definition
is not of hope so much as of what we aptly term 'wishful
thinking'.

If there is no reasonable expectation of the fulfilment of what we think of as hope, the act of hoping is really destructive to peace of mind. If we say: 'I hope that will come off; I think it *will*,' we are really hoping because we apparently have grounds for expectation of fulfilment. If we say: 'I hope that will come off, but I *don't* think it will,' we are actually saying something without very much sense in it. And I say, hope is an oddity in philosophy.

And yet, who of us could get far without it? Just that tiny flicker, the minute electric spark within which moves us on a bit from where we might otherwise stop a long time, which makes us think there is always something in life worth striving for, something worth the effort to have as our very own. Hope warms the soul. Hope takes us on, year by year, until the end - which is only the beginning. Hope is born in us; it never quite leaves us. *And the surest hope we shall ever know in this world is the certainty of the next.*

Perhaps it is because the sense of hope is so often crushed by disappointment that it is such an oddity. It is difficult to say; but philosophy does *not* teach us that going on hoping, in spite of disappointment, is the best or the only cure for the effect of the disappointment.

Philosophy is always simpler than that. It teaches you and me that the prime factor in dealing with the effect of the disappointment is to *disallow* it. If we continue to admit, after the first shock of a disappointment, that we *are* disappointed, the sense of disappointment will not leave us. It is only when our complexes rise in all their superiority that we even begin to break down our reactions. If we disallow disappointment we do something towards our peace of mind by clearing a space in our minds to receive such peace. We have to remember that peace of mind is not a minute sensation; it has no sharp point to it. Quite on the contrary, it spreads like a vapour and needs to be allowed to *expand*. To obtain, and retain, peace of mind there must be no jealousies, no irritabilities, no valueless sighings, no harbourings of a sense of frustration.

But, on the other hand, no slackness of mind. It is impossible to lay enough emphasis on that fact. A mind quite blank is a mind distressed. The more virile the mind, the more we think objectively—and projectively—the more prepared is the mind for the entry of peace.

To let the mind go slack, to give up thinking (beyond what one must do merely to exist) is to set one's self in opposition to the whole idea of the soul. It is to quarrel with the soul; and the man who is not at peace with his own soul, which should ever be driving him on to something worth while, is not at peace with the God who gave him that soul. A tranquil mind can never be his.

Disappointment where others are concerned can be a serious cause for disturbance of mind. The nearer and dearer they are the graver the disappointment.

In children not least. Children do not always turn out as we imagined they would. A child may become something we never desired, or not become something we did desire; or have developed tendencies we do not approve, even regard with definite dislike. We may be forced to accept the fact that our own child has inherited many of our bad points and few of our good. Whatever may be the actual form of cause, we suffer disappointment. What was the good (we say) of lavishing our love, and of having taken all the trouble we did take to turn him or her out really well? It may be the man she married, or the girl he married, who is the prime cause of our disappointment. It hardly signifies; such disappointments are common enough.

It is no hard or unbending philosophy which insists that each of us is an entity, that we are neither our brother's nor our son's keeper; or that if we allow thoughts of dissatisfaction and disappointment to assail our minds—and remain there—because of what our son is, or our daughter is not, we are shouldering a burden *and calling it a burden*.

Let us shoulder any burden we must, but let us set our complexes high and cease to regard it *as* a burden, which means we are simply adding the *thought* to the *fact* and bearing more than we need bear.

'Bear one another's burdens' was a command of Christ who seems to have spent his time doing little else; but nothing he said teaches us to sacrifice our peace of mind over it. Bearing the burden of others is a magnificent act; it becomes less magnificent if we let them, or anyone else, know how heavy the burden is. Even if others *allow* us to bear their burdens, even if they are *content* to let us bear them, it is the same—except that we may have to consider whether bearing such burdens is worse (or better) than throwing them down and suggesting they should pick them up. There is always a limit to personal endurance, and we may have to choose between enduring or refusing to endure; but if the burden *is* endured, the powerful mind seeks to hide its personal estimate of the weight of it.

The bitterest disappointment where others are concerned must surely be caused by the thought of the fallen idol. The husband she worshipped, the wife he adored, fallen from their high estate, their feet of the poorest clay. Are we to be expected to disallow such a disappointment (should it be ours) and proceed as though it had not been? What about philosophy? What about the once-brilliant superiority complex? What can either do, now that the bottom of the whole world has fallen out? Has not our flaring indignation been justified? And the agony of jealousy we have gone through—has that not been warranted also? The heartbreak we have known . . . and now the idol at our feet, smashed beyond repair.

Philosophy has an answer even for that. Peace of mind depends primarily upon power to forgive the seemingly unforgivable. It hangs upon power to clear the mind of anger, jealousy, even righteous indignation. Much has been said and written about that kind of indignation, but no philosopher (as far as I am aware) has ever tried to insist that even *the most righteous* indignation does not disturb peace of mind.

It is a question of values. If you or I have been in agony of mind because we have seen an idol crash, we have to decide whether or not we shall go down under the grief of it or whether we shall rise superior to that grief. It is not a question of our personal grief at the time; it is a question of life as a whole. We have only one life to live here. if we are going to live too much of it grieving, when we come to review that life with our Creator the period when we let grief conquer us will present a poor aspect.

It has been said that God never tries any of us beyond endurance. That is true, but it really means that God gives to each of us the chance to endure; if we take that chance with a complex set high, peace of mind comes to us automatically; if we refuse the chance or delay before accepting it, the complex itself becomes automatically set low. None of us can afford to let that happen. We do a grand thing when we adopt a slogan from the poet Heine who wrote the words of Schumann's *Dichterliebe*: 'Ich grolle nicht—I shall not grieve.'

And that epitomizes the whole thought of a tranquil mind in spite of disappointment. To clear the mind so that peace can enter it—and stay there when once it has entered—means providing the mind with a space cleared from thoughts of the wrong kind. Unforgiving thoughts take much space in the mind; thoughts of retaliation probably take more space still; but a tranquil mind means filling *all* spaces at once and in such a way that the power to think acts in full force. That is why a tranquil mind is of such vital importance to us while we remain on earth; that is why life here is life *without* a capital L unless a tranquil mind is ours.

Time heals, they say. Of course, because time is a power; but if you grieve or fret, and expect time to heal you of your misery, you will have—just another disappointment.

Yet because of the sweetness of the Maker-of-time you find that (as His time goes on) your mind becomes more and still more at peace, you can take the fact to mean that your complex superior is fast approaching the state of being a complex supreme. You will derive satisfaction from what once may have caused you misgiving; you will be pleased with your own virile thinking. Just as life itself is a going-on process, so is the tranquillity that should accompany life. As it is certainly true that you and I pass this way once only, it is as well that we do a few jobs for other people while we are here. That alone is enough to dispel much of the effect of disappointment we ourselves may have suffered.

If .we think that way, disappointments begin to shrivel up almost as soon as they are born. Instead of dissatisfaction, there is a chance of being satisfied with what has come our way. When, at last, we have come to the end of that way we may feel like agreeing with the Psalmist when he said: 'But as for me, I shall behold Thy presence in righteousness.' We can even add under our breath (as he may have done) 'and when I wake up after Thy likeness, *I shall be satisfied with it.*'

XII

A TRANQUIL MIND IN SPITE OF REGRETS

Weep no more, nor sigh nor groan;
Sorrow calls no time that's gone:
Violets plucked the sweetest rain
Makes not fresh, nor grow again.

So wrote the notable Fletcher of Saltoun. His calm philosophy shall make do for my text in this chapter in which I intend thoroughly to examine the ideas suggested by the term *regret*.

An unsatisfactory word in some ways. It has not even an inspiring lineage. It merely comes from the French verb *regretter*. The French themselves admit its origin is unknown, that it has no interesting family tree to expose. As for its meaning, it can boast nothing better in the philosophical sense than a chain of unpleasant and somewhat futile thoughts in: 'Sorrow and pain due to reflection on something one has done or left undone.' As for the expression 'vain regrets', one is left to wonder whether regrets are ever anything except vain.

At all events, regrets must be classed among the negative conditions of life; they do no-one much good. Penitence and repentance are not necessarily negative because the suggestion in both is that one has at least tried, or has thought of trying, to make amends for an injury done. I make this observation because the difference between the condition of being penitent or repentant, and that of being merely regretful, goes deeply into philosophy. Penitence and repentance are both positive conditions of mind in that they both amount to contrition implying desire for amendment; regret is wholly negative because no such desire is implied. Philosophy takes a poor view of anything wholly negative, and it is only when we turn our regrets into something a trifle more positive and virile that they cease to be regrets.

The act of regretting is a state of mind resultant from continual, or periodical, wishing we had or had not taken a certain course of action. (The expression 'course of action' must here make do for thought, speech, or movement, of any kind). The whole idea of regret is that we took a certain course of action and that our peace of mind is still disturbed by the thought of it. In other words, we are filling the mind with thought-impressions taking up so much room that peace—which, as I have said, spreads and requires space to go on spreading—is being first compressed and finally ousted. That is poor philosophy because the tendency of mind is weak; we have gone the wrong way about those violets Andrew Fletcher spoke about.

We have plucked our violets (by which he means we have committed our mistakes) but we have failed to appreciate that not even the sweetest rain (our tears of regret and chagrin) can ever make those violets grow again—in other words, *can undo the mistakes*. If we persist in keeping the violets we plucked, pressing them between the leaves of our Bible so that we can still look at them, we do a vain thing. We merely offer permanent sanctuary to something that should have had a time limit set for it.

That is what regretting comes to: offering permanent sanctuary in the memory to something better forgotten. The consequence is always the same: *disruption of thought*. And where there is disruption there cannot be peace.

Harbouring thoughts of regret has much the same effect as harbouring those of resentment. Indeed, in a sense, regrets are resentments—against one's self, of course. If we harbour them we are our own disturbers-of-the-peace, and therefore our own worst enemies. We hurt our own souls. Our complexes are likely to droop in consequence. Everything about us and our thinking drops below standard. We have, spiritually, nothing much to say for ourselves. We are like the Psalmist at his lowest ebb: we are 'poured out like water'. All our bones are 'out of joint'. Our hearts within us are 'like melting wax'.

We do a better thing to take a square look at the situation and to examine what it was we said, or did, that still casts a cloud over our best thoughts and discolours everything we look at. If we have come by the worse of it, personally, there is nothing to be gained by reminding ourselves every other minute that had we not taken that particular course we should not be in our present plight. The hard fact remains that we *are* in that plight, but only a complex inferior will cause us to make things worse by nursing the memory of it. Not even the sweetest rain will cause the violets we plucked to grow again; but we can do worse than remember that violets are not the only flowers to cultivate.

If we continue to offer sanctuary to thoughts we had better banish, we are actually picking more violets. In a few years' time we shall have such a collection of them, carefully pressed between the leaves of our Bible, that we shall run the risk of damaging the edition—or, at least, its binding. Our regrets will be so many and profuse that we shall be in the unenviable state of *regretting our regrets* as well as the original cause of them. We shall then be in a worse condition than ever was our friend the Psalmist who seems to have been so vulnerable that he was high up one moment and flat down the next. What he wrote— apart from some of its extreme beauty of language—is worth reading in order to prime our own minds against ever getting into the state he found himself in when things went wrong with him. Jesus admired the Psalmist, whoever he may actually have been, but it is noteworthy that the Son of Man spared us quotations from his most pessimistic moods.

That reminds me to observe at this point that the if-I-could-have-my-time-again type of thought is *the really useless* thought of all negative thoughts. We can never have our time over again. If we did have it, we might be like the people in Sir James Barrie's *Dear Brutus* who each had theirs again. And how did they get on? What did they do the second time? You will remember that they did no better than they did the first time.

Connecting the effect of a mistake with the actual cause of it is wrong, philosophically. All causes have effects, but that is no reason why we should always combine them in our memories. We do better to leave the cause and tackle the effect. If an effect we have caused has brought us unhappiness, we are not likely to miss a similar cause another time. We shall agree with old Æschylus who said it was disgraceful to stumble against the same stone twice. If our stumble caused (and possibly still causes) someone else to suffer, the same thing applies. Our action was the cause, and he bears the effect. That is, admittedly, much worse—but still, in spite of it, we do something unwise (and we act in direct opposition to the laws of philosophy) if we continue to connect *our* cause with the *effect on him*. Instead, it is for us to do our best to put right what we originally made wrong. Even if circumstances forbid our approaching him, even if he has never forgiven and never will forgive us, it is still possible to do something to make up to him.

Thoughts are powerful agencies, and a mind powerful enough to project thoughts can do a great deal. If we have that person in mind periodically—even only for a few seconds at a time—we can do much to atone for the mistake we have made. We can remember that there is a Supreme Power, and that by projecting thought towards that Power, *with that man's image in our mind's eye*, we can do more than may have been hitherto dreamed of in our philosophy. The more we flash the ether for power the more certain are we of making up for a mistake; but if we persist in connecting our remedial work to the original cause of it, we merely harbour a regret. And that will *not* add to our peace of mind.

Fletcher's violets can also represent the mistakes of

omission as well as of commission: the only-if-I-had-remembered-to-do-that kind of mistake. The thought reminds me of the story of the dear old Victorian lady who paraphrased the general confession in her bedside prayers: 'I have done those things I ought not to have done, and have left undone those things I ought to have *done up*.' Her complex must indeed have been low; at all events, she is credited with having eventually committed suicide because there was 'so much buttoning and unbuttoning in life'. And yet she was right in laying emphasis upon her sins of omission, for such sins often bring to life a very acute form of regret—largely because such regret is attended by a feeling of intense irritation. It depends on what it is but (particularly if it happens to be the cause of letting someone else down) it has the negative effect of making us feel we cannot forgive ourselves.

It may be we omitted to say the right word at the right moment and caused offence by the omission. The impression we gave, by not saying anything, put us in a false position. No matter which way it may have been, the same methods of dealing with it hold good. We all know how true it is that in this world, where the rules of society often militate against our being really sincere, we are sometimes prevented from making good such damage as we have caused.

If our apology is made, and refused, we have sorrowfully to withdraw; but our peace of mind should not thereby be disturbed. We have done what we could and, in any event, it is the other person's mind which is disturbed. Knowing that, it is our privilege to make a thoroughly good job of it; it is for us to project thoughts of a kindly nature towards that person. Because he has refused to forgive us is no reason for us to set up a fresh chain of thoughts directed against him. On the contrary, philosophy would have it that the least we can do is to conclude the matter by projecting kindly thoughts in his direction.

That is acting according to the laws of simple philosophy; but if we lose our balance at that point and begin to go over the whole affair again, piecing its little bits together and making of it a solid lump of regret, *we have spoilt our good job*. We shall not get the peace we feel we deserve.

It is the same with almost any kind of regret. We may regret we went there when we should have done better to stay here; or the other way round. It is all one, philosophically: we are killing our peace of mind by linking causes with effects. If we acted on someone's advice or gave advice (and wish we had held our tongues) it is just the same. There is only one way to deal with it: tear out the memory of the cause and deal with the reality of the effect.

> It is the cause, it is the cause, my soul—
> Let me not name it to you, chaste stars!

wrote Shakespeare in *Othello*. Neither you nor I can afford to name the causes of our regrets too often. If we are to have a tranquil mind in spite of regrets, we must deal properly with the regrets in order to have a tranquil mind.

Regrets are never more poignant than when they concern memories of those who have left this world. Many a man and woman has endured the suffering of the damned through having harboured regrets connected with those loved—and lost. Yet such regrets are, by their very nature, utterly vain.

If you or I have lost someone for whom we could have done more than we did, with whom we quarrelled when we might have been at peace, against whom we said much that need never have been thought (let alone said), from whom we took so much and to whom we gave so little, over whom we exerted an influence not to our credit, for whom we now entertain feelings of respect we failed to show while he was here—our peace of mind may reasonably stand in jeopardy.

Yet, surely we did *something* for him? Was he appreciative of what we did, or did he just take it all for granted? His attitude must come under analysis equally with our own. If we quarrelled, one of us had to end the quarrel. Did *we* end it, or did we leave it to him to do so? If we said things against him, were all our unkind speeches unpro-

voked? Perhaps we forgot to show him the respect he was
entitled to and our present regret is bound up in the thought
that he is no longer here? If he were, we say, it would be
different. Possibly it would, but we cannot have him back
again. We can repeat Swinburne, and recite what he wrote
in memory of his friend Inchbold:

> For if, beyond the shadow and the sleep
> A place there be for souls without a stain,
> Where peace is perfect, and delight more deep
> Than seas or skies that change and shine again;
> There none, of all unsullied souls that live,
> May hold a surer station: none may lend
> More light to hope and memory's lamp, nor give
> More joy, than thine, to those who called thee friend.

Yes; we can say all that—but we cannot bring him back.
All the same, it is for us to remember the powers vested
in our soul. It is now a question between us and that soul,
which is the same thing as saying between our soul and the
Giver of that soul. It is a serious matter: one that requires
thoughtful dealing with.

Even where the acutest remorse is concerned there is
always something to be done to get peace of mind in spite
of it. So often feelings of remorse are not really justified;
but if the remorseful person thinks otherwise, who are
you or who am I to bully him into what we consider a
better way of thinking?

If we ourselves have hurt someone, now dead and
therefore beyond recall, it is plainly impossible for us to
approach him to ask his pardon. Then it can only be a
matter between us and our Creator. It is in the very nature
of things that the Supreme Mind, understanding man's
thoughts 'long before', will be delighted to accept the
slightest gesture on the part of one of His earthly creatures.
If we failed someone by doing less for him than we might
have done, and we register a vow *never to fail anyone else*
in the same fashion, our peace of mind can be assured *the
instant we make that decision.* The very making-up of the
mind in this way brings with it a sense of peaceful relief.

Should we have caused quarrels or refused to make up

those caused by someone else, the answer is exactly the same. The very instant we realize that it is not worth while to quarrel as an individual member of society, when the nations of the earth hardly ever cease quarrelling, *that very instant* can be a turning-point in our experience.

If our regret has been because of something we said about another person no longer here, the same philosophy holds good in the sight of the Supreme Philosopher. By His own laws, relief of mind comes to us the instant we realize that saying unkind things about another person is something to avoid, if only because it is so general in what we are pleased to call our society.

It is indeed an elementary philosophy that prevents any of us asking for what we do not like; but, in the broad sense, it is equally philosophical to receive with gratitude and to give because we receive. If we have taken without gratitude from someone now beyond our reach, philosophy teaches us that if our minds are disturbed at the thought of it *we can in future give graciously* and with a mental blessing to go along with the gift.

If it is the question of our personal influence, the antidote to mental unrest is just as simple; but, perhaps, a little graver. Each of us exerts influence just as each of us absorbs influence. None of us can afford to disregard the effect of our influence. The Victorian type of piety—quite reasonably, I think—had much less influence than its creators imagined it would have. Be that as it may, that particular type of influence cuts little ice these days. We have passed the period in history when it was thought wicked to whistle on Sundays.

To exert an influence is to cause something to *flow in* from where *we* stand; but such flowing-in is rarely successful if we *set out* to be an example. When we do that we run the risk of giving the game away. We are deliberately adopting an attitude, however commendable it may be; moreover, we are acting a part. We need to be first-rate actors if we are to disguise the fact. We are likely to be detected in what may be a splendid act, but which is instantly rated as an act in a play rather than one in real life.

But to return to remorse in the circumstances in which we have been considering it, our peace of mind stands in jeopardy *not one second* after we have appreciated that if we exercise influence, no matter how or over whom, we undertake responsibility. It is the same if we serve anyone, employer or otherwise. Philosophy insists that service on our part should be rendered to our employer in such a manner that the Creator accepts that service *as though it were rendered directly to Himself*. We all serve one another in some way; that is the law of our world. Many of us profess to serve God, but not all of us realize that honourable and unstinting service to a fellow-creature means serving God *through that fellow-creature*. If such simple philosophy were more widely accepted, service itself would be raised to its real dignity. It is said that the King of England is the servant of his people, and few will deny it. It might even be true in a sense that the King of kings is good enough to serve you and me; indeed, it seems very like it when we come to think of all He allows us—*and saves us from*. It is a simple thought, but true philosophy is nothing unless it is simple.

Lastly, there is the question of respect—of regrets because we did not value someone until after his death, especially when we failed to respect someone whom others did respect. This brings up the whole question of what is termed 'respect for the dead' for review. Plutarch commented on what Solon had written on the subject, thus: 'That law of Solon's is justly to be commended which forbids men to speak ill of the dead.' And we all know the Latin tag '*de mortuis nihil nisi bonum*'—'concerning the dead nothing unless good.'

To begin with, Solon's philosophy was at fault—at least, if he meant his statement to be read and taken literally; moreover, Plutarch should have known better than to commend him for it. If *we* are to carry out Solon's idea we may as well begin early with Nero and finish late with Hitler. Have any of us ever said much that is good about the latter, for example? If we say only what is good about the dead we fail in our judgement. If the dead we

speak of are known to us personally, it is better we
speak of them as though they were still living and in our
presence. If we carry out some such principle as that we
are not likely to go far wrong; we shall then make a habit
of speaking of the recent dead as though they were part
of the history of our time.

After all, the lives of all of us are part of history. We may
be modest enough to think our own lives are an unimportant part, but even if we do think that way we can still
pay respect to the lives of others who have moved about
in the pages of our own history. Still, judgement is judgement and Solon's ideas were basically wrong because, if
they are stretched ever so little, they are likely to amount to
complaining of our relatives or friends while they lived
and eulogizing them after they have gone.

To examine the whole thought of regrets, once more, is
to conclude that they are vain; and vanity is a poor thing
at the best. Ecclesiastes took a dim view of life when he
said that *everything* was vanity, and no modern philosopher
would listen to him. Everything is *not* vain. If it were,
there would be no such thing as the superiority complex
for any of us to make use of; everything would be rated at
the lowest value.

Neither was the writer of the Koran correct in his judgement when he observed that 'the present life is no other
than a toy or a plaything; but the future abode of paradise
is life indeed.' Nothing could be further from the truth.
If that *were* true life here would lose its value. This life is
no plaything; only a fool regards it as such.

I have just thought of another statement, but whether
it was Arthur or Edward Young who wrote it, I am not
sure. Anyhow, whichever it was, wrote: 'Vain is the world
—but only to the vain.' He was nearer the mark.

Life is not vain; only its regrets are vain. If we persist
in harbouring regrets our peace of mind becomes a vanity
in itself. If we thus allow every fraction of peace to escape
us, our lives will then very definitely become one long
vanity. It is for us to deal with our regrets according to
the laws of simple philosophy and to keep our complexes

highly superior while we do so. If we do that—in spite of the most poignant regrets—peace of mind can be captured and held.

We all pluck our violets; but to expect them to grow again is but vanity. Or, changing the metaphor, we all spill a little milk on our journeys; and we all *know* the vanity of crying over it. Simple philosophy suggests that if, as we trudge the road of circumstance, we chance to spill a little milk *we had better step over it and not look back*. There is more milk we can buy, and we can take more care with it. But what has been spilt has gone.

The next shower of rain will wash it away.

XIII

A TRANQUIL MIND IN SPITE OF THIS WORLD

I ONCE knew a family who allowed politics, and the world situation in general, to ruin their happiness. The head of the family was a socialist first and a father second; his wife evidently felt it to be her duty to produce a number of little socialists, which she certainly did. I know I thought the baby might turn out to be an anarchist.

When the children grew up they ate politics with every meal. I was actually told that they addressed one another as 'Comrade', but I am not prepared to say that this is a fact. But I do know that they wrangled about politics with anyone who would wrangle with them. The eldest girl became the Senior Wrangler of the neighbourhood. When election-time came round, members of that family who were qualified to vote did so with such vehemence that it is a wonder they did not cause a miscount.

A tranquil mind must have been something they can never have valued, even if any of them actually understood the meaning of the expression. They always gave one the impression they had just been asked to pay the national debt. Most of us avoided them. I must confess I did so:

but my excuse is that when I passed any of them in the road-
way I found myself suddenly becoming conscious of the
political situation. I felt instinctively that there must be
something wrong with it, and wished I had read my paper
a little more closely and found out what it was. That family
oozed politics from every pore; they almost sweated socialism.

I think they must have been exceptional, for I never
came across another family like them. And yet you yourself
must be able to make a short list of people you know who
are tainted with the same thing. Any one of us may fall
into the habit of allowing world politics to disturb our
private peace of mind; but if we do, we are acting in opposition to most forms of philosophy.

It is not only a question of politics. I merely brought up
the subject because I happened to think of a family of
amateur politicians who so palpably worried—and probably still worry—about the world situation. The result
affected their whole outlook on life. They adopted that
attitude that, whether God is in His Heaven or not, there
is nothing right in or with the world. If you had known
any of them, and had gone so far as to make an observation
of an optimistic nature, it would have been met with a
sentence beginning: 'yes, but . . .'

A family of *yesbutters*.

We all meet people who will tell us that England is
'finished', that nothing will ever be the same again. The
obvious answer is that, after a major war lasting six years,
it is *impossible* for things to be the same. Added to which is
the thought that, in some respects, it may be better not to
have them the same.

Whichever way it be, the philosophical principle of
never allowing thoughts of a disturbing character to assail
the peace of one's mind, merely because there is strife
everywhere, is a principle worth following. At all events,
the Son of God must have thought so; otherwise it is hard
to understand why he bade his closest friends to be of good
cheer, despite world conditions.

The question of a tranquil mind in spite of this world,
and its strife, lies in our ability to view the world (outside

our own little world) in reasonable perspective. If we view it with all sense of perspective distorted we shall atrophy every thought of a happy day spent in it.

Adolph Hitler did that. He thought of nothing but subduing the world. Even if (just as an argument for the moment) we grant him that his ideals were mistaken, and nothing worse, we can never believe that he enjoyed a day of his life in this world. Of all men of modern times, he must have known least about peace of mind. What were his thoughts before he took his own life we shall never know; all we can conjecture is that such thoughts cannot have been those of peace. No-one who seeks to disturb the peace of other people's minds can expect to have peace in his own. Having said that, it seems to me that it will be necessary to work out a few multiplication sums before you or I can get any real idea of what must have been the state of mind in a man who disturbed the peace of the whole world.

It has been said that uneasy lies the head which wears a crown. Perhaps so, if the king persists in trying to sleep with his crown *on* – but not otherwise; at least, not necessarily so. The king who loves his people, and who is loved by them, should wear his crown easily enough. Only when kings were despots and ruled by force, ever disturbing the minds of their peoples, did they find their crowns uneasy in the wearing.

The thought is enough to remind us that what matters — far more than the great world at large (unless we happen to be prime ministers or foreign secretaries) — is our own little world and what we can make of our lives in it. When Christ told his disciples that they were likely to have tribulation in the world, he meant in their own little world. He must have meant that because he knew none of them would ever rise to power and become rulers-of-men. What he said to them he might have said to you and me. It was after he said it that he added the injunction: 'but be of good cheer; I have overcome the world.' Though the chapter ends at that point, he may actually have gone on talking and have said much more than has been recorded. It does not strain our imagination to think he may have added that any of *them* could overcome the world in the sense that tribulation, however bad it might be, need not disturb their tranquillity. I am inclined to think that something of the sort *must* have been in his mind—and theirs—because he had just been telling them that 'these things I have spoken to you that, in me, ye might have peace.'

How wonderfully serene was the mind of the Son of God! Heaven knows he had enough to put up with. Yet, thinking of him as a man only for the moment, his complex was so completely superior, his nature so calm and reposeful, that he seemed capable of raising the very *value* of peace every time he spoke of it. Minds like his can do that kind of thing. His mind was just *filled* with peace. Because of that he turned peace from a *condition* into a *power*.

The fact is that we can all overcome the world in the same way that the Son of God overcame it. It may be true—indeed, it *must* be true because he said so—that he came not to send peace but a sword; but that was because he knew man would never accept his precepts and not fight over them. He knew that half the wars the world would go through would be over religion. He must have known that some of them would be called crusades, a word with the etymological suggestion of a *cross* in it. And yet—he himself was called the Prince of Peace.

If you and I have peace about us, as he had, we can take what the world has to offer us in the fullest stride. We can go ahead with our purposes, we can go where peace is *not* and come away unaffected and undismayed; we can know what it is to be spiritually fearless.

Fearlessness and peace are often companions. Any of us may be fearful or timid by nature, even though our ideals may be high. If we analyse our impulses we may find we are taking a certain course partly because we fear what the world will say if we take any other. However honest in soul we may be, we shall find that this really comes to something like keeping our hands from picking and stealing because we fear to come within the reach of the law, not because we know it is wrong to steal. So long as we do not steal, it would seem that either way of thought will do;

but if spiritual fearlessness is to be ours, it is not in accordance with philosophy to modify it with fear of any kind. A nice point, but one worth thinking about.

Another point about spiritual fearlessness is that it can never be mistaken for the fearlessness so often associated with callousness. No philosophy teaches us that we can sail through life fearless of everyone we meet and without regard for what they may think, feel, or say. If we do that it will be as well we do not drive a car, for we are certain to join the ignoble army of road-hogs.

Yet, if we take to heart everything our bit of world has to say about us—or we imagine it says about us—peace of mind is not likely to be ours. The best thing we can do, if we are in danger of that, is to recall how we regarded what the world said when we played the game of *consequences* in the days of our childhood. We shall then remember how we contributed to a vivid account of him who met her; where they met; what they were wearing; what he said to her and she to him; what the consequence was. We shall also remember that we terminated this crudite contribution to the world's literature by recording *what the world said*.

When I played it my world usually said 'Rats!'

Perhaps yours did, too? But you came to the same conclusion: that it did not matter all that much what the world said. It certainly cost neither of us a sleepless night.

In spite of what our world says, or does not say, philosophy says we must overcome our world; we must proceed on our way through it with our complex highly set. If you or I are to make a mark in our little world, it is for us to see that it is a mark worth leaving. If it is only a dirty mark, the least we can do is to spend time (which we *should* be spending to better advantage) erasing as much of it as possible. It may never be our privilege to set the Thames on fire, but so long as we set nothing else on fire that will burn disastrously where others are concerned we can afford to regard Father Thames as a peaceful personality and *leave* him at peace.

Yet should it be our privilege and good fortune to be a

favourite in our world of acquaintances and friends, we can do worse than be grateful for the warmth of their friendship. If our world is really large and our audiences many in number, our complexes should be correspondingly superior because if our heads get turned and we begin to fancy our position to be *higher* than it really is, if we fancy our world is *larger* than it really is, we are rather like the so-called 'well-travelled' person who takes pride in leaving labels on his travelling gear in order to impress others who have not travelled. That, by the way, used to be a very common form of the inferiority complex when travelling was so general before the advent of war restricted it.

Yet, again, we are *who* we are; there is no philosophy in our pretending we are *less* than we are, merely to give the impression that we are modest or unassuming. It is only when we seek to give the impression that we are *better* than we really are that we go wrong in the philosophical sense. If we steer clear of such snags we need never sleep badly at night for thinking of what the world says.

Probably it says nothing more intelligent than 'Rats!' anyway.

XIV

A TRANQUIL MIND THROUGH CONTEMPLATION AND STUDY

To *contemplate* may mean 'to look at with continued attention' but that is not to suggest the process is necessarily long. Far from it, because to contemplate is also to view closely, and presumably with judgement and criticism. Such criticism can be formed in a flash, especially when we have had the advantage of previous experience. Contemplation, in that sense, is definitely the forerunner of accurate speed, without which very little in this world can be obtained in the way of technique.

To acquire 'technique in contemplating', owing to the way the mind is constructed, begin by keeping quiet for a few seconds—indeed, until the first stray thought comes your way. By following up the thought with a chain of thoughts—no matter whether the actual thoughts are of high value or not—it is possible to indulge in an act of contemplation which can be regarded merely as a rehearsal.

As a variation of such rehearsal, quite a successful method is to read something worth while and then to think over what has been read, referring to the text in case anything has slipped the memory. By thinking over the impressions gained from the reading it is possible to set some hundreds of them. That kind of treatment the memory likes. It likes as much of it as you are good enough to provide it with. Perhaps what Richard Wagner said is true: whatever is worth reading at all is generally worth reading twice.

It is not everyone who can honestly say he remembers all he reads. Half the trouble is that he has often been conscious of other things, or of other people, while he has been reading. You yourself must have often had the experience of trying to read while others were talking, and of finding yourself reading the same paragraph three or four times without taking in a word of it. After a year of intensive practice in the fashion I have suggested you will lose yourself. in a book, no matter how much noise other people are making. It is only a matter of practice, and it is a grand thing to be able to do.

The value of good and intensive reading hardly needs pointing out; what can be suggested is this: the act of thinking over deeply what you have read is in itself a peaceful action to which the mind readily responds.

The same thing applies to listening to radio transmissions. If we switch on and leave a programme to its own devices, especially if we do it habitually, we merely allow radio to constitute a noisy background to our home lives. It is extremely doubtful whether radio then has any value at all. Yet one imagines there must be something to be had out of it because so many people do that; but it is clearly outside the realms of philosophy to suggest that entertainment is really entertainment *unless* it is attended to.

But there is far more than this in contemplation considered as a philosophical experience. There is a great deal to be had out of letting the mind rove until it comes into line with something worth thinking about. Particularly if it is something to do with the immediate future. Thinking last thing at night over something we shall do first thing in the morning—just a calm, reposeful chain of thoughts—puts us in a splendid position, mentally and spiritually, when we come to tackle the morning's work. So many people rely on taking everything at a moment's notice; so few people really *prepare*. In this respect the view of the most successful musicians can be taken to heart: they never perform in public anything they have not rehearsed in private.

It is all part of the same philosophy which teaches us that what has been prepared is likely to come off better than what has not been prepared. Our daily work, and its hundreds of details, must be important to us because by it we earn the right to live; but if we adopt a policy of never giving it a thought from the time we leave it at night until we are back at it the next morning, we act in direct contravention of the laws of philosophy. Quiet contemplation of our attitude to our life-work is a stimulant to the mind; as a consequence the tendency of that mind rises more and more superior to the work. The result is increased peace of mind.

Work itself is not always peaceful. It may so happen that your own is not. You may have to endure noise from the moment you begin until the moment you stop; you yourself may have to make some of that noise. If that is the case, you are to be forgiven for the deepness of the sigh you heave when you leave the scene of that work; all the same, sighing is a bad policy because one sigh seems to deserve another, and it is a pity if you awake with a sigh because you went to sleep with one. The noise of your noisy work will begin to sound in your ears long before you have finished breakfast.

' If it means an effort of will to stand up to the conditions work ' imposes, that work does not in itself contribute towards peace of mind. That means our only chance of being at peace occurs when we are away from work.

Philosophy has a word to say for that. If we devote a little time (especially at night before sleep overtakes our senses) in contemplation of the conditions work imposes, we do much to strengthen our resistance against those conditions. There is no question of steeling ourselves against anything; it is only a question of projecting peaceful thoughts into our work and the conditions such work imposes. Practice is everything; in time we shall find ourselves far less conscious of, far less irritated by, the conditions—however bad they may be.

Intellectual pursuits feed the mind and burnish the memory. Deep reading, study of one of the arts, active interest in some literary theme, study of the thoughts of other men, all combine towards the forming of our own thoughts and opinions, and make of us lovers-of-wisdom.

We all learn from one another; that is why it is so important to study the thoughts of others. Mere experience of life, though it teaches us much, is not enough to keep a healthy mind going at white heat and top speed. A brain that is slowing down is slowing down everything with it. Every action we make, every movement we are responsible for, is the direct result of our thinking. If we allow our thinking machines to slow down we are offering resistance to the action of our immortal souls; it is hardly sound philosophy which causes us to do that.

It is not even the barest common sense. If we have taken the trouble to work up our speed of thinking it is hardly a good policy to slacken the screws that have held our thinking together all these years. So long as we never let go of things intellectual—so long as we read, remember, and study, as a daily habit—we shall never go downhill in the spiritual sense and we shall do much to prevent ourselves failing in the physical sense.

In the work of maintaining the mind often lies its peace. There is something essentially peace-inspiring about deep learning. For that very reason we often find real scholars are the most peaceful of men. Temperaments vary; but it

is none the less true that scholars are often calm and
tranquil. To my way of thinking it is not in the least
surprising because, if any of us is intent upon learning
anything that has to be absorbed by study and research,
we automatically become quiet in mind. The brain becomes
daily more penetrating; the reflexes sharpen; the eye
becomes more accurate, the concentration higher. Perhaps
the last-mentioned fact is the most important of all where
a tranquil mind is concerned, for if we learn to concentrate
perfectly no disturbing thoughts can pass through the brain.
It is so worth while. With perfect concentration the world
fades out for a period, but we come back into it refreshed
for the delightful experience of having been out of it.

Seeking solitude is not the only—or, indeed, the best—
way of acquiring peace of mind; but it is *one* way. To seek
peace of mind through solitude and deep study *alone* is a
mistake. We are here to live our lives with our contemporaries, and there is no philosophy that teaches you or
me to shun our fellow-creatures. If we do that we shall
be held to account for it; even if we are not, we shall realize
how much more we might have done by being with others
and doing something for them. All the same, to enter a
room and shut the doors is a grand thing to do periodically.
In such hours of solitude we can view everything connected with life here in something like true perspective,
and with the inevitable (and extremely satisfactory) result
that our personalities grow in power. We learn to give
out much of what we have taken in.

Much knowledge can come to be ours if we make it a
habit to pursue some form of intellectual hobby. We can
never know enough, or even half enough; but the more we
do know the more we shall want to know. The realization
of how little we know is the first sign, often enough, of our
tendencies rising towards the superior, *and so on towards
the supreme*. This last condition really does mean that we
know, who we are, and why we were sent here. It is grand
knowledge, when it comes, because we appreciate all that
life can possibly mean. And if we allow our minds to pass
out of this world now and again, and let our contemplation

and study lift us towards the Supreme Himself, we may find that in the silence of solitude we are actually least alone, and that He (who never began and who never can end) *personally sends* us our peace, saying: 'Be still, then, and *know* that I am God.'

XV

A TRANQUIL MIND THROUGH THE POWER OF PERSONALITY

IN 1914 it was said that if King Edward had been alive the Kaiser would not have risked going to war. That may or may not have been true; but the fact is recognized that personalities whether of emperors, kings, statesmen, or film-stars, have always influenced the hearts of men. Thinking of King Edward's great personality, it is amusing to remember how he (as we say) 'went to pieces' when summoned into the dread presence of his mother (Queen Victoria) in order to account for something he had or had not done. Personality again.

Such examples are admittedly extreme; not all of us are kings or queens. The principle is the same, for all that. Moreover, most of us are quick to recognize power in a personality when it is there to recognize. We miss very little in that respect. We become so accustomed to detecting power, or the lack of it, in people we even only glance at, sometimes, that we quickly form elementary estimates of them. Getting to know them is likely to improve such estimates; often we sustain the shock of considerable surprise. Men we took to be really powerful we discover to be blusterers with a highly-developed inferiority complex; men we took to be meek and mild prove to have developed the superior complex, and have a distinct way with them. Between these two extremes can exist all manner of means.

Our own personality is something we should enjoy reviewing occasionally. It hurts none of us to look in a mirror and be critical over what we see there. Is our expression hard and disdainful, or is it the expression of

someone who has an occasional thought for others? We
may be plain or even ugly, or we may be the reverse; we
may not have a decent feature to bless ourselves with, or we
may possess looks that would make a Greek god envious.
Our height may be sufficient to make our presence com-
manding; or we may be so short as to appear insignificant.
It may be quite the other way round: we may be so tall
that our height *detracts* from our bearing; or we may be
short, but give the impression we are live wires and know
what we are about.

And our voices? There are not too many pleasing voices
in these islands. The trouble is that so few of us are taught
to use our voices, with the consequence that we misuse
them every time we open our mouths.

Speech matters a great deal. We have only to listen to
speakers who broadcast to appreciate that. They are entirely
dependent upon our ears to establish their personalities
merely because they are invisible; only those who have
attained some mastery over English inflection can hope
to hold our attention for long.

Movements also matter. Films prove that to us. If we see
a topical film, in which ordinary people are moving about,
we recognize at once that training is necessary for perfect
effect; we know that is so because we see accomplished
actors and actresses who have learnt how to move before a
camera. It has been said that, on the whole, the personalities
of the British people are passable. Yes—until we see some
of them run for a bus; then we are not so sure.

Grace of personality—the combination of impelling
facial expression, an attractive voice, fascinating movements—is not the possession of all of us; but those who have
it have a very great deal. Characteristic modes of expression
carry much weight, a fact easily proved by listening to one
or other of these amusing impersonators who broadcast
from time to time. One I can think of, in particular, can
alter his voice and manner of utterance to such a degree
that it is indeed hard not to believe he is the person he
imitates. I know I have often fallen to wondering whether
the person imitated is listening and, if so, what his reactions

are. The very fact that impersonating well-known people forms entertainment at all is a good proof that personalities matter; otherwise there would be no point – and certainly no entertainment—in imitating them.

And yet, the real personality—what actually lies behind all we see in a person—is something which may not be imitated—at least, in any form that can be appreciated. All you and I can value in anyone's personality is the *effect* of it. The cause of that effect is the person's own affair, and is strictly private. We may admire a man for his sweetness of character, his utter integrity, the kindly advice he gives so unstintingly—but all these things are effects, not causes. The causes lie deeply hidden. They lie within that man's soul.

The question of the power of personality with regard to a tranquil mind is a two-sided question. The first—at least, I propose to take it first—is what we extract from the personalities we come in contact with and know best. If you can think—at this moment as you read this—of someone whose personality has a quiet charm about it, you will agree that to be in his or her presence is a pleasurable experience. At the same time the thought of someone very different may occur to you, and you realize that to be in his or her presence is *not* pleasurable. If you quickly call to mind the personalities of half-a-dozen people whose images come before your mental vision at this moment, you will agree that you have six different sets of thoughts about them.

People affect us. The more we know them and what we call 'their little ways' the more distinctive we find the several effects they produce where we are concerned. We may also recall the several effects they produce on others in whose company we are likely to find them.

The real question is: how far are we going to let them affect us adversely? If we have already made up our minds not to let *anyone's* personality affect us, we must have developed yet another form of the inferiority complex because we are virtually steeling ourselves against *all* personalities. In other words, we are making an attempt to stand alone. We become the type impossible to get to know.

We hack our way through things without regard for anyone else. We are posing, which means we are not sincere. Insincerity in any form is part of the lower complex. Unfortunately, the very effort of striking a pose is enough to disturb our real peace of mind—especially if we fail to create the impression we set out to create.

That is where the superiority complex comes in so neatly. If we have it, we shall be eminently approachable. If we allow others to approach us—if we attract them so that they *will* approach us—it is often possible to obtain much in the way of peace from them. Naturally, there are the other kinds to deal with; not everyone radiates peace. Yet the superiority complex is a tendency of mind that causes its owner to respond to a similar complex in someone else. Like a bee who knows his business, he extracts the sweetness and leaves the rest.

The other side of the question is the more important because it concerns what we have to give out. If we are unreliable, and fail our friends and associates, their sense of regard for us falls like mercury in the tube of a thermometer. The resultant sense of chill invades the senses of all concerned—first, the friends and associates; *but no-one can produce a chill without himself feeling it.*

If our personality is what is called the fiery kind we may produce heat when it is least wanted, and our most tolerant friends may be compelled to stand more from us than we deserve they should. A fiery temperament, in itself, is no part of the inferiority complex; but it is also true to say it is no part of the complex superior. It is an *ex*treme never like to become *su*preme.

It may have a damaging result in that our more timid friends may secretly be afraid of us. Should we detect the fact, we are in danger of open attack from still another form of the complex inferior—one that may bring out an older sense which should have been suppressed at school, when the temptation to bully a weaker personality may have been acute. It is a very thin line that divides such situations. In any case, our bolder friends will not be afraid of us; they are quite likely to bait us. That means a tranquil mind will be further away from us than it need be: being baited in any way has a knack of reproducing unpleasant reflections.

A fiery temper and a strong temper are by no means the same thing. The former causes ructions all round; the latter looks all round before causing the ructions.

If we are reliable and sound, our personalities quiet and serene, a double power flows from us because our complexes must be approaching the supreme; if that is the case, we are capable of handling the most delicate situations to a nicety. The power to do that *certainly* brings peace of mind and contentment of spirit, merely because the results obtained are so gratifying. Such personalities are actual forces; such personalities are irresistible—especially to those whose own powers are less impressive and strong. If ours is a personality of that kind we are bound to be social successes, which means we are also bound to enjoy the returning flow of peaceful thoughts from those who know us for what we really are.

If we can make peace where there is likelihood of trouble, if we can prevent trouble in the sense that no-one is likely to risk causing it when we are about, we must be sending forth such vibrations of peace through our splendid thinking that nothing but peaceful vibrations are returning towards us. It is by the laws the Serene Himself made that, if our own serenity conquers the turbulence of others, we wring from them *still more power for ourselves* without leaving them the weaker for it. It is for us to win a victory over a social rioter without reading the riot act. If there is a grumbler abroad, it is for us to fascinate him until he either swallows his own grumbling or loses his grumbling technique. It is always possible to overwhelm a grumbler with the power of personal serenity; if you or I can do that we must indeed be approaching the complex supreme. That cannot mean anything *except* a tranquil mind because, in spite of natural laws acting against us as well as for us, if we are *anywhere near* the complex supreme we are absorbing *all* our power from the Mind of the Supreme Himself. To get to that stage may not be easy, but it can always be done; each of us has an equal chance of doing it.

To get to that level of thinking is superbly satisfactory because one is so much on top of things; one has a real sense of mental power. If, as a result, any of us makes a success of things in the financial sense, we shall have the right to enjoy the power wealth always gives to those who acquire it. We shall do well to remember that Moses of old strongly upheld such power, so long as men kept their balance. 'For', said that humble old soul, 'it is the Lord thy God that giveth thee power to get wealth.'

Moses must have been one of the first to sense the danger that so often encompasses marked personal success of this kind, but I am quite sure he was not the originator of the saying that money does not bring happiness. Moses would have said that happiness is just what it *should* bring. He knew, as well as anyone, that creature comforts are not to be despised. He mixed with rich and poor, and appreciated their respective positions. What he thought then is what we should think now: in a world where currency and coinage exist, money must be the most important mundane consideration––merely because it is impossible to live without it. Moses would have been the first to agree with that, even if he sagely added: 'but it is not impossible to live *above* it.' Neither is it, if a man's soul is generous.

A mean person knows little peace because meanness in itself is an enemy to peace. If a person is mean he suffers in two ways: first from his own thoughts and actions; second from the thoughts of others. Of the two, I am inclined to think the latter is the worse, from his point of view, because no-one can ever think of a mean person *generously*. One is put off, defeated. If a man is really mean, it takes a generous mind indeed to credit him even with such meagre generosity as, in his best moments, he possesses. Giving a dog a bad name and then hanging him is never more applicable than to what happens to a man who is mean. Even his friends give him a bad name; his acquaintances' do the hanging.

Power of personality is so well worth striving to acquire; it is so greatly *esteemed*. Only those who are jealous of it affect to despise it. Such power has to be gradually built up;

it rarely comes without conscious effort. It is actually the outward manifestation of inward grace—in other words, it is the outcome of a man's entire thinking, the outward expression of his soul. And when that soul goes on, after life here is done, the personality (which was the outward sign of that soul) is sadly missed. It is also reasonable to suppose that the entry of that same soul into the life beyond is joyously welcomed.

The thought is enough to furnish yet another proof that all men are not equal. If they were (or were so considered to be) on their entry into the planes of the Eternal there would be little reason to try to develop power here. It might then not even be true that man is judged on his motives in life; and if he is not to be judged on them— and possibly them alone – it becomes increasingly difficult to decide what he is to be judged on, or whether he is judged at all.

Yet judgement there must be; we have been warned of it. If a man has been a creator of peace, he must have known peace of mind. Judgement on that part of his actions in life must be hardly more than a comment by the Judge: 'You created peace; peace was yours. Let us pass on to something else.' That 'something else'—for you and for me, when our time comes—may well be *any creation of our own*.

Anything we create here is the child of our brains. It may be a picture we have painted; if so, that picture is part of our thinking. It may be a building we have designed—perhaps only a simple rock-garden we have fashioned out of something we happened to have by us; even so, it is our creation; it reflects our thinking. It may only be a letter we have written, but it is our creation; it shows our manner of thinking at the time we wrote it. Every effect we produce has a cause behind it—in our minds. That is why we are judged hereafter on our motives.

If, where we are in a position to command, we express our commands in such terms, and with such inflection, that others feel it *a privilege to obey them* we are making our own personalities directly responsible for peace all round us; we have learned the power of radiation. We have realized that radiation is *driving* (round and round) some kind of power.

There is another thought about radiation. It is *not* driving in a straight line: that is propulsion. Radiation is always concerned with circles. To radiate peace and good-will is to project both in such a manner that we ourselves become a central point of power. And, by the laws of the Giver-of-peace, every time we cause rhythmical vibrations of peace to radiate in circles round us, those vibrations obey a law of nature. When we are alone we shall realize that those same vibrations have *closed round us*. What we have done for others has been done for us—and by the action of God's laws. The vibrations we have set in motion have gradually come to rest about us; but, before they actually ceased to vibrate they (so to speak) finished off their job by reacting upon our own consciousness. That happens to anyone who radiates peace.

If we think for a moment of the state of mind in a murderer, we shall think of what has often been described as the 'murderer's dream'. This is generally thought to mean that he sees his victim and goes through the scenes of his crime again. His mind is being seared by the vibrations his own evil has set in motion.

Actually the same set of laws comes into force whether we radiate evil or good, strife or peace. The effect is different, but that is not surprising. It is a very simple philosophy that comforts us with the lovely thought that if you and I radiate nothing but peace we have nothing to fear from any law made by the God of peace.

The peace we radiate will reach us again.

XVI

A TRANQUIL MIND THROUGH POWER
OF LOVE

No philosophy, however simple, can be quite complete without including a study of the power of love—for power it certainly is. That it is an emotional sense of attraction felt for one person by another or, in the more extended sense, a similar emotion towards an impersonal object, is good enough for the dictionaries and is true; but it is a bare definition, for all that.

Love was originally based upon universal instincts; it still exists in a rudimentary state noticeable in the parental affections of the lower animals. But, during the course of ages, love in man himself has become something very much more complex; it has long since comprised highly spiritual and moral elements.

Love has had a long and somewhat strange history. Strange because it has often been mixed up with war and hatred. In the days of savagery it was love that inspired a man to fight for his home, for his mate, for his children. It was love that made him attack the homes of others so that he could add to the creature comforts of his own. As man developed, he found himself belonging to a race instead of to a tribe; later still, to a nation instead of either. And, because of that knowledge, man has learned the meaning of love of his own fatherland, an instinct that has never left him.

It was because of love that man first made his laws. They were the elementary laws of his society, and they protected both him and those he loved. Among those laws were some that governed everything to do with his marriage and home-life; indeed, he regarded such laws as his most important.

It was in the earliest days of his existence on earth that man first developed love for inanimate objects. He made things for himself and his home; gradually, his love for such things formed the basis of his technique in fashioning them. After that he soon began to love making them because he found he could go on making them more and more beautifully. From that grew man's love of art.

At first, his attempt at art was crude and rough; gradually, as the centuries went on, his attempts at portrayal of what he loved best progressed; the flat appearance, so noticeable in early drawings and sculptures we have managed to preserve, began to disappear. Man had begun to appreciate the laws of perspective. It took centuries before he actually realized that parallel lines appear to meet in the distance, but when he did find that out he made a very different job of his pictures.

Music, as an art, is comparatively modern. The laws of harmony, counterpoint, canon, and fugue, did not exist in any organized form before the sixteenth century. John Sebastian Bach, a century later than that, crystallized them and gave us our first notable polyphony. Love of the beautiful was the driving force behind everything he, and other men like him, strove for.

The conception of love has held a prominent place in more than one early system of philosophy. Perhaps the most interesting—and also one of the most ancient—is that of the Greek philosopher Empedocles.

A somewhat strange philosopher; but his philosophy has always appealed to me, and certainly suits my purpose at the moment. If I find in him much that was previously suggested by Pythagoras, I find much more that was eventually developed by Plato and Aristotle. I confess I am not deeply thrilled by Empedocles when he tells me there are four 'ultimate elements' in the form of earth, air, fire, and water; but I begin to revive my interest in him when he tells me he considers that these four 'elements' are really four primal divinities of which are made all the world's structures, and that they are eternally brought into union, or eternally parted from one another, by two powers— Love and Strife. When he tells me anything like that I cheerfully forgive him his faulty science out of regard for his having lived in Sicily four centuries before Christ; moreover, I find his thoughts about Love and Strife uniting or parting everything else in life the basis of an excellent and simple philosophy.

Poor old Empedocles! The Sicilians thought the world of him. To them he was the perfect statesman, prophet, and physician. The power of his personality was amazing. It seems (by the way) that he dressed for the part, too. At all events, the Sicilians regarded his august appearance with reverence and love; and he himself was delighted to move about among them magnificently garbed in purple robes bound by a golden girdle, with brazen sandals to match. (Those sandals, incidentally, are worthy of note, for a reason to be given later.) Altogether, he must have presented an imposing appearance with his long hair bound up in a delphic garland—and all those slaves following him wherever he went.

Still, for all his pomp and circumstance, his philosophy was always about love. The Sicilians thronged in hundreds to hear him say that the four great elements were held together by love. So far as they were concerned, he could talk his head off—so long as he talked about love. They listened to every word he uttered on the theme and then formed little discussion groups among themselves.

Empedocles talked more about love than any man has since—except the Son of Man himself. It is unlikely, however, that he was the originator of the saying that 'love makes the world go round' because he lived much too early in the world's life to have thought that it either *went* round or *was* round.

Perhaps it was his phenomenal success that turned his head in the end. It takes anyone all his time to preserve a perfectly balanced mind after finding himself rated as a demigod. One's complex must indeed be superior if one is to take that kind of thing and not slip a cog or two. It may have been so in his case. It may have been that he found it difficult to deal with the popular belief that he had been responsible for the marshes round Selinus becoming sufficiently salubrious for people to go and live there; or it may have been that he felt a little upset on finding himself credited with having quietened the winds that ruined so many harvests round Agrimentum. Perhaps he found it more than he could do to play the part, even if he succeeded in dressing for it. At all events, the rest of his story is sad.

It appears that a great feast had been held in his honour. One would imagine that such an occurrence was fairly frequent. Whether his digestion was out of order or not must remain a matter of conjecture—but he suddenly disappeared. Demigods, however, cannot disappear in, that unseemly fashion without inquiries being made. They were in this instance; but all that could be discovered was that Empedocles had been called away to Jupiter. And to Jupiter he had gone in a blaze of light.

As a matter of fact, he had *not* gone to Jupiter even though he must have encountered the blaze of light. He actually climbed up Mount Etna and jumped down the crater. The truth of this might never have been known—but for those brazen sandals. Had he been wearing leather shoes, or carpet slippers, Etna might have burnt them up when she burnt him up; but the lady evidently disapproved of brazen footwear. At all events, she rudely belched them up and deposited them outside. They were subsequently found.

Some of the more discerning amateur philosophers in Agrimentum, in discussing the event, found it hard to decide whether the demigod had developed what corresponded to their notion of the inferiority complex (which would have amounted to his feeling unable to live up to his reputation) or whether he sought to establish for all time their theory of transmigration of souls by means of what appealed to them as a wonderful act of deceit. Whichever way they decided, they never ceased to honour the name of Empedocles. Even as late as 1872 the followers of Mazzini revered him as 'the democrat of antiquity'.

A pity he went like that because he had stumbled on the truth that everything worth while in this world is bound by Love and parted by Strife. At times Plato's ideas about love followed those of Empedocles quite closely. He thought that passionate love in man and woman was the shadow of, and a preparation for, the soul's love for the eternal ideas of what is only good and beautiful. Love, in Plato's philosophy, seeks only love—and always finds it. As for the soul, being (these are his words) an *idea* or *immaterial substance* it seeks only complete union with the beautiful.

•From which it is safe to conclude that if Plato had realized that his soul was his power to think, his philosophy would not have been greatly changed. But he never got quite so far as that.

The thought of man expressing love for his Creator never entered the minds of the early Greek philosophers. The reason for this is to be found in Greek mythology. Jupiter and Juno, for example, were supposed to be King and Queen of Heaven; but their domestic quarrels were a byword. Even the Goddess of Love—the great Venus herself—was credited with being almost insanely jealous. In those early days men had not begun to realize what a God could be. It is therefore not in the least surprising to learn that the Greeks could not found a philosophy based on the love of man for his God. Such a conception was entirely alien to classical antiquity.

On the other hand, there are traces of the beginnings of it in various eastern religions. In many forms of Hinduism something of the kind is found, but it was the Hebrew prophets who really first associated love with God in the idea of the love of Jehovah and Israel. That (and the thought of mutual love 'twixt man and wife) actually led up to Christianity, the first-and-only-*demonstrated* revelation of divine love.

From all this sprang love in its most exalted form. Yet we can still afford to believe just a little in poor old Empedocles who was so convinced that Love and Strife were personalities that ruled everything. For six bitter years Strife had it his own way, but not to the exclusion of Love. It was the love of God Himself that made men go to save their fellow-creatures and gain their posthumous V.C.'s in the doing of it; it was love that sent men from their homes to fight against an enemy who only knew hatred; it was love that actuated the minds of women who nursed such men back to health under appalling conditions; it was love that made the people of London (and elsewhere) go out into the blackness to help others whose homes were destroyed. Empedocles would have said—had he been here to say it— 'What did I tell you? The two greatest forces in this world *are* Love and Strife.'

There are many forms of philosophy that idealize the

power of love. Pantheism, as a good example, teaches that love is the mainspring of the universe. There are others, far too numerous to sort out here. Neither is there any need to sort them out; all that matters for my purpose is to insist that *love is a power*.

Because love is a power it acts like one. It, and it alone, has the strength to quell strife. The war which ended in 1918 proved it. How many of us said at the time—and have said since—that we ought to have gone on into Berlin! That would have meant a further loss of life. It was love of humanity which made November 11 a day of remembrance.

That love is a power has always been obvious; the world's history alone has furnished the proof. If we think once more of man's home thousands of years ago, and how he sought to protect and keep it inviolate for those he loved who shared it with him, we appreciate the power of love. Love was the power behind all man's early quarrels with those who sought to interfere with his liberty or that of his wife and family.

It is just as true to-day. Love in the home is the greatest power the home can ever know. What is home without love? What is home where there is eternal strife? The power of love is so great, and so enveloping, that it unites its own power with the most ordinary actions of man's brain. If we possess the real power of love, and possess also the superiority complex, we shall be almost infallible when it comes to warding off strife in the home. The quality we thus display is commonly called tact, but there is more in it than saying a seasonable thing at the right season for it. The power behind all reasonable and seasonable speech is the power of love.

If the blessing of God is ever to rest upon a marriage it can only be when the partners in that marriage see to it that their love is never allowed to dim its own brightness. Love should always be expressed because it thrives on expression. Only by expression can it grow. The man and woman who give up expressing what they were (at one time) so ready and eager to express, are taking the first step towards dimming the brightness of their love.

We have only to think of a few families of our own acquaintance to realize how varied home conditions can be. I am thinking of several at this moment. I can recall vivid memories of a family where love can never have been expressed, though I am sure it actually existed. The members of that family would have given their lives for one another, but love was something never expressed or even hinted at.

It was a family of tempers and temperaments. If Empedocles had known it he would have declared that because there was so much strife there must also have been love. I do know that it was positively a dangerous proceeding to go to that house without having previously given full and due notice; one was sure to come upon one of the girls in tears, or one of the men roaring with rage—and yet, out of their home, every member of that unhappy family was attractive and completely charming. Again, they thought the world of their home—at least, you would have thought so had you visited them at Christmas. I did so once and thoroughly enjoyed the day, even though I was a trifle taken aback when one of them said, late in the evening: 'Thank goodness Christmas is over for another year!' And, to be honest, I must record that when I visited them at Christmas, three or four years later, I found them quarrelling furiously over their Christmas presents. . . .

But they were loyal to each other. The only possible conclusion I can come to is that such love as I never doubted they really felt for each other *was* a power, but a very secret power.

If an Englishman's home is really his castle it should also be his shrine, his sanctuary—where his love is expressed. The married couple who adore one another—*and are not afraid to say so*—fully realize the power of love. To revert to mythology for a simile is to suggest that the child Cupid brings a quiver full of his brightest golden arrows, and practises archery by shooting them into those people's hearts. That mischievous little god, so often a random archer, would seem to be taking his archery seriously for once. Perhaps he feels snug and warm in an atmosphere of love and contentment. Perhaps he likes being the god of love, and flatters himself that his accurate shooting means that love will breed love, that love always fosters love, that love *crowns* love—and so generously! And the little god of love—the son of the beautiful Venus—may enjoy the thought of his human targets being great lovers; he may commend them for their wisdom, even if he fails to realize Whom it is they address when he overhears their sincerest and deepest prayer: 'Grant we may be sweethearts to the end'.

Only those who live their lives surrounded and enveloped by the power of love are likely to carry that power outside their homes. With the best intentions in the world it is difficult in the extreme for a man or woman, whose home is a place where love is weakened by strife, to carry the power of love about with them. It can be done—it *has* been done—but it is not easy of accomplishment. The thought of strife at home, of unceasing irritability, of constant disagreement, remains with all but those whose complex is so superior that they are capable of effecting a complete metamorphosis immediately the home gate is latched behind them. Even then there is always the consciousness of having to return and unlatch that gate; there is always the chilling thought of the reception he or she is likely to be accorded. Yet, if the complex is high enough, such an entry can be effected quite safely. The power of love, in the end, always wins.

And if we ourselves are the means whereby the power of love does win in the end, long before that end is reached —and by the laws of the God of peace—there will be peace in our own minds.

The mental sensation of what is called *gratitude* provides an excellent illustration of a further piece of simple philosophy I should like to put before you at this point. Gratitude, you will agree, must be a form of love because it is actually a warm feeling of good will towards a benefactor. Ingratitude, the opposite condition of mind, is an indisposition to acknowledge benefits received.

My purpose here is to try to show how much easier it is to appreciate the sensation of gratitude than it is to appreciate the sensation of love. If we love a person we are supposed to have kindly feelings towards that person. At rock bottom no doubt we have; but there is a condition of mind, usually brought about by jealous thinking, which will cause a lover—one who loves—to retain feelings that are anything but kind. Hence, of course, what is generally known as 'the lovers' quarrel'. So that as the sensation of love is not always a sensation of peace or serenity, it is a little more difficult to analyse. But with the sensation of gratitude there is no difficulty at all. It is a sensation we can call to mind and thoroughly appreciate because of its simplicity. The sensations of love are many—and much more complex.

Gratitude, as a sensation, proceeds from a mind at least temporarily at peace. That is not always true of love. It is impossible to experience that sense of good will (which we call gratitude) with our minds disturbed. There may have been disturbance only a moment ago; but the sensation of gratitude must, the next moment, dispel such disturbance. Because of this, it becomes another point in simple philosophy to suggest that the sense of gratitude should be permanently associated with the sense of love. In other words, to cultivate the general sense of love, combined with that of gratitude, is to cultivate something that *must*, by its very nature, bring peace to the mind.

It is no poor philosophy to insist that a sense of gratitude, deliberately cultivated, is turned from a mere virtue into a power. Linked with love it is bound to become one; that is obvious. By itself it is merely a virtue—indeed, there is a very ancient proverb (probably of Greek origin) which would have us believe that 'gratitude is the *least* of the virtues; ingratitude is the *worst* of vices'. I quote that because it is rather quaint, but I am not inclined to say I think either part of it is philosophically sound.

Whether we believe that proverb or not, we should all agree that gratitude is a grand sensation. I might have said a 'grand *experience*' and not been wrong. It really is an experience. If you or I have had the misfortune to walk along a lonely road in a bitter east wind, or a blinding snowstorm, and find a room with a blazing fire in the grate and a hot meal waiting us, the experience is extremely pleasing. The warmth and the meal account for much of it, but there is also the peace of mind that is ours when we are even vaguely grateful for the fact that we have a home, that we have a fire in it, and that there is a meal to eat. Even if unexpressed, the sense of gratitude is there. We have only to picture the reverse to appreciate it: a cold room and no meal, even though there is still the house, will hardly have the same effect.

So that gratitude is an experience and worth regarding as such. To walk through our own garden and be thrilled at the profusion of its flowers is a pleasant experience, but it is only partially made up of pleasure at the sight and scent of those flowers ; even if unexpressed because it is not actually realized, *part* of the sensation of pleasure emanates from a sense of gratitude because the Creator has provided flowers for man to cultivate.

Where philosophy comes in is where we appreciate the value of gratitude as an experience, where we deliberately allow ourselves to be attracted by it. We all like to repeat experiences we enjoy; knowing that, the philosopher suggests we enjoy the experience of gratitude by deliberately repeating it. If we regard everything we enjoy as a blessing we can make a good beginning by being grateful for our blessings, whether we are mathematically-minded enough to count them, each as a unit, or not. The philosopher's contention is that, as gratitude is an experience that must bring peace of mind, *it is an experience worth designedly repeating*. We have often said: 'I am too grateful for words'; the reply of the philosopher is that no words are necessary, except when expression of gratitude is being made to some-one else.

The wordless expression of gratitude is, more often than not, a mere flash on the ether; and, by the laws of the Giver-of-all-things, an answering flash comes back. It will be in some form of power to the mind, perhaps just an increased sense of peace in the mind. It is quite likely to be that because, by God's own laws, gratitude and peace of mind were ordained to go together.

There is one further thought about gratitude. It is gratitude for the life of someone who has left this earth to live elsewhere. A simple, but quite deep philosophy, governs the course of one's thoughts here. The question arises as to how much we are justified in mourning those who have left us. Philosophers of olden times would have considered it our duty to mourn our dead; or, if they thought otherwise, not many would have risked unpopularity by saying what they really did think. Modern philosophers take another view —at least, most of them do. Modern philosophy is inclined to suggest that we mingle our tears at our loss of those we love with a sense of gratitude for their lives here, the more so when such lives were exemplary. Gratitude to the Giver-of-life for what He has permitted us to enjoy *because of the life of someone dear to us* is a courtesy to Him and an experience for us. It means that we have appreciated all that loved person was to us. If that appreciation is expressed in gratitude for his life here, the answering flash on the ether (from the God who has called him away) means less poignancy in our grief and greater peace of mind.

The other form of love embraced by the later philosophers—love for the Creator—is one I am not prepared to deal with to any extent as a question of religion; this book does not deal with religion, as I have already said. As a form of philosophy, however, I can approach it, even though (now I come to think of it) old Socrates would have stared at me in amazement for suggesting that there could even *be* such a form of philosophy. Socrates was proud of his word *philosophy*. He actually coined it. He was proud to think he had added a grand word to the Greek language. Philosopher—a lover of wisdom! It suited the good Socrates' to think he was that.

Apart, then, from any question of religion—even though Christ taught men to love God because He Himself is the personification of love—there is a philosophical side to this question. If our philosophy embraces the recognition of a Supreme Being—which, of course, it must—we actually offer love to the Creator every time we express love for anything of His creation. If we love the mountains and the sea, the woods and the valleys—if we really do love the experience of being within sight of them—we combine our love of, and our gratitude for, these things; we then transmit our experience to Him by means of our thinking. And because we love what He made, we actually offer love to Him as the Maker. If we love all that great music, great art, great architecture, mean to us—again we offer our love in the form of gratitude to the Creator who put the love of these things into the hearts of men capable of bringing them to perfection. From the purely philosophical standpoint, whether or not we worship that God in public, following the course of some form of organized religion, is neither here nor there. Probably we do, thus combining our religion with our simplest philosophy. In so doing we certainly unite two ideals that will never break apart.

We began with the thought of a tranquil mind through power of love. Let us return to it, convinced that love is the crown of life. If we lose the technique of keeping the gems of that crown bright and brilliant as once they may have been, a dimness comes over the crown and over the place where the crown is kept. Love is then no longer expressed because there is so little point in expressing it. Love may still actually exist, but there is no *definition* about it. It is— how sad in the saying!—merely Love-in-a-mist.

If we forget how to forgive, or how to make good our mistakes, we miss much in life. If we have hitherto taken everything for granted we have *already* missed much in life. A tranquil mind has not been ours. We have missed the fact that love need never be Love-in-a-mist. Love cannot thrive in a mist. It must always be kept warm—and mists are chilly. As Love-in-the-light it will thrive. Then it really blesses; it does what Portia said mercy did: it blesses him that gives and him that takes. It must be so because it is the only quality about us humans that can be said to approach the divine. And none of us can ever believe that the Divinity of God is not love. Nothing is so divine in man, nothing so near the heart of the Divine God who made man.

But Love-in-a-mist is Love-made-to-suffer. It is Love-hardly-alive. That is why philosophy teaches you and me that love must be expressed if it is to survive. It is one thing to awaken to the hard fact that love is still in the home, but is shrouded in a thick mist; that is bad enough: it is quite another thing to awaken to the harder fact that the home, far from being a haven of peace and contentment, is only a place where Love lies a-bleeding.

EPILOGUE: THE PASSING HOURS

THUS far I have said nothing much about age. Naturally, I have no knowledge of yours—except that I know you must be in one or other of the seven ages of man.

The first three years of anyone's life here is babyhood. It has to be regarded as an age altogether separate from its successors because no-one retains any memory of it. If you think this out you will agree that you yourself cannot recall anything (with any certainty) which happened to you before the age of three. If you do remember anything—it will only be faintly if you do—the reason is probably that you were told something soon after you were that age, and it is *that fact* you have remembered. Broadly speaking, anyhow, it is true to say that none of us can remember anything which happened before we were three.

From that age until, roughly, fourteen is childhood. The actual period differs in individual cases because it is determined by the bodily change known as puberty. By English law no-one (except a member of the Royal Family) is regarded as having attained majority until the age of twenty-one; but from every other point of view a boy is a man, a girl a woman, on reaching puberty; both are then capable of reproduction.

From fourteen to twenty-five is best regarded as the age of youth. From twenty-five to forty is early maturity; from forty to fifty-five is late maturity. From then until seventy is prime.

This last statement may cause surprise because prime has so often been considered a much earlier period in life.

Physically, in the athletic sense, that will do; but I am not thinking of that. This book is all about thought and thinking, and I maintain that from fifty-five to seventy a healthy person is still in prime, by which I mean that he is at the height of his mental powers. I think the lives of most really great men prove the statement. In some people prime ends before seventy, at which time in their lives they enter *age*. Even then it need not necessarily be *old* age. I think those divisions will stand up to a fairly searching test.

It has been stated that man's expectation of life in this part of the world is round about sixty-two years; a woman's, apparently, is thought to be slightly longer. In the statistics themselves I am not particularly interested; what interests me far more is my discovery (largely through reading biography) that, providing they have lived *beyond* sixty-two, the world's greatest thinkers have done their greatest work at this very age. The great painters, the writers — and certainly the composers — seem to have been at their peak at sixty-two. That is what makes me think that sixty-two is well within the period of prime. If a man dies at that age he is generally considered to have died in the prime of life.

Even with the idea of prime not ending until at least seventy, one hesitates before making a definite statement as to whether or not a man or a woman should retire from a life-work ; or, if so, *when*. No two cases can be alike. Some men find retirement brings a relief of mind; others seem hardly to know what to do with themselves. I speak from no personal experience: I have not retired — nor am I thinking of retiring — but the idea of retirement interests me even if the experience of it might bore me.

To my way of thinking, the attitude of retirement is most at fault when a person adopts the soul-take-thine-ease style of procedure. We all remember Christ's parable about the man who adopted that style. He imagined he was in for a grand time: instead, he died. Such an attitude is paramount to addressing one's power to think and giving it a hint to do no more thinking. Rather like immobilizing one's engine, surely? A somewhat weak ending to a life of activity.

The whole point of retiring must lie in a change of activity, not in a stopping of it. If you or I retire with the idea of anything less than a change of occupation, if we retire with the intention of doing nothing much with the rest of our lives, what have we left? *Just old age.*

And that is never worth having. After seventy we may be within the period called 'age', but anything which may be accurately defined as *'old* age' need never be reached at all. If we have spent years of life in the thoroughly healthy occupation our work has given us, if we have also absorbed power from its only true Source, we simply cannot stop being active in mind. Our days in age will be as vivid as those in prime.

Anyone well past the age of seventy may say to himself at this point: 'It is all very well for him to write in that strain; when he is as old as I am he will change his tune.'

I have an answer for that. Leaving out the question of impaired health—which must *always* be the exception—a life of great mental activity (in the sense of what I have been describing) demands continued mental activity. The act of absorbing power is much too fascinating to be lightly given up. Once any of us has become clever at it, he will *never* give it up. He will just go on, right to the end. And his mind will be at peace.

The converse is not pleasant in the contemplating. Giving up first this and then that, merely because one imagines one is too old for it, will never enter a mind accustomed to absorbing strength from the Source of it. In saying that I do not suggest any of us can learn the secret of eternal youth; as far as is known, there is no such secret. It is doubtful whether it would be divulged if there were. But a mind tuned up as high as it will go is a mind that *gives up nothing* Age is something no-one need fear; it is old age, and all it may mean, that any of us might reasonably fear.

The thought reminds me of my intense amusement at a satirical remark made by a friend when my wife showed him a photograph of her and myself. He said he thought the likenesses good. I said I thought the likeness of my wife was decidedly good, but added that I looked 'like a benign old gentleman'.

'That's a bit hard on you', he said. 'The trouble is that, as you are neither benign *nor* a gentleman, there is only the old part left.'

At the time I chuckled at his tartness, but it has occurred to me since that his philosophy was sound: if one retires and lets things go, only the 'old part ' *is* left.

Age, if allowed to assume the appearance and properties of being old, is likely to be little else. Often enough it is a pitiable condition. No doubt you can think of friends of your own who have—perhaps quite suddenly—become really old, and have obviously lost their grip of things. On the other hand, you can bring to mind elderly people who are—as everyone who knows them says—'wonderful for their age'.

But *are* they so wonderful? Are they not just what they should be? Why must they be considered the notable exception instead of the ordinary rule? The answer is quite likely to be that they have discovered the secret of absorbing power. Not the secret of eternal youth, perhaps, but the secret of *deferred old age*. A tranquil mind will be part of that secret.

Whatever may be the actual cause in any particular case, we need never doubt that anyone who has spent time in being conscious of the Supreme Power has found his life a vivid experience. It is impossible, by the laws of that Power, for anyone who has lived a life of quick, concentrative thought to become prematurely aged. The only exception is that of serious illness or of generally-impaired health—but (as I have said before) that is the *only* exception. All the same, he who has become clever at absorbing power (and the phrase is not amiss) is likely to keep fitter than he might otherwise. Even if the worst has happened, and he has become the victim of something serious in that way, he stands a much greater chance of overcoming it. He may, indeed, be 'wonderful' for his age. If so, his mind *must* be at peace.

In any event, 'age' is a relative term. 'Old age' should not be a term at all. If a life has been an ever-increasing absorption of power, the height of that power is only reached *at the end.* That is where a true climax should come. Where else would you have it?

If a man reaches an age when he has no longer any need to earn his living he is in a grand position. Hitherto his time has not been his own, but his employer's. Even if he has been his own employer this is in a sense true: his time has not strictly been his own. If he is able to retire and live in peace for the rest of his days he has all the time there is. A grand thought, provided he has gripped the real secret of age.

That secret lies in a realization of the passing hours. The hours go on passing because that is their job; but it is never any part of *our* job to let them pass without taking note of them. The days are full of hours just as the hours are full of minutes—and all days are important. If we regard our own days as important and keep them full of minutes, which themselves are well filled, the years will not matter. That gets us all out of being dubbed *well stricken in years*.

Age, then, just remains a somewhat vague and wholly a relative term. By the time we have reached it we should thoroughly appreciate the value of Christ's suggestion that there is no need to take too much thought for the morrow. If we realize that this life is a preparation for the next, and that time saved here is time saved hereafter, we shall continue with our healthy occupation of filling and ever-filling our minds, knowing that *over*-filling them is an impossibility. We brought a good deal into this world, and we shall then take out a good deal more than we ever brought in with us; in the meantime we shall have acquired a tranquil mind.

It is a comfortable thought that none of us is ever asked to go before our time is up. Then we are sent for; not one second before. The power to think came as a flash and at a given second in time; the same power leaves the body behind it at a given second in time. The Maker-of-time alone is responsible for both occurrences. Age does not come into it. If it did, we might all live exactly the same length of time.

It is not uncommon to find people fearing death. Occasionally one detects the fact. If we fear death the whole meaning of life is lost. It must be, because we have admittedly failed to grip the basic fact that death is a bodily affair; it has nothing to do with the soul—which *never* dies. Death is merely a journey effected in a few seconds. We ourselves have no responsibility connected with it. Even what we take away with us is not packed up by us; it is packed for us by the laws of nature. The fact that death is feared at all is actually the complementary conception of what we call human nature. (The accent is heavily on *human*.)

If we were not given the tendencies and instincts common to all living creatures here, we should rapidly degenerate into a nation of suicides. The will to live, as exemplified in the saying that 'a drowning man catches at a straw', is something every sane person possesses. Upon this fact is founded coroners' verdicts, so often to the effect that suicide has been committed during temporary unsoundness of mind; but minds that *are* sound cause their owners to cling to life. Minds that are sounder still, because they have been trained to the utmost, cause their owners to regard death as *an incident in life*.

So long as we appreciate what we can do for ourselves by training and using our powers to think, we can face the simple change from life here into life there with perfect calm and equanimity. Our consciousness of the passing hours means that our minds continue to reach out until the end comes here, and the next second—the beginning comes there. We shall never cease to reach out for more and still more knowledge; we shall continue to fill the passing hours, knowing that it is never too late to learn. We shall realize that—during the passing hours—we are nearing our real climax, our real height of power. We are being wise enough to keep the climax until the time comes for it—and, as I have said already, that is at the end.

I have called this chapter *The Passing Hours*, but I have allowed my pen to run away with my thoughts, and have been writing as though my title had been *The Hours Have Passed*—or, at least, have *almost* passed. But they have not yet passed—either for you or for me. Moreover, they are only passing at their normal speed. You and I are still in the throes of this grand life here. The stress still lies on the importance of thinking for us both; but such stress, being in the right place, in no way interferes with our peace of mind. . . .

*   *   *   *   *

I have already twice quoted from Maeterlinck's fairy play *The Blue Bird*. You may have actually seen it, either when it was originally produced in 1911 at the Haymarket Theatre with incidental music by Norman O'Neill, or when it was revived in 1921 and ran for a few seasons at various London theatres with my own incidental music. Conducting performances of it, night after night for weeks at a time, naturally gave me a memory-knowledge of the whole play. I always liked it, but I never thought it was quite suitable for young children—at least, not by comparison with Barrie's *Peter Pan*. I remember that we had to modify incidents in *The Blue Bird* we considered likely to frighten very young or excitable children.

There was a scene (known to us as *The Graveyard Scene*) which really needed more modification than it actually received; but there was a wonderful curtain-line to it. Maeterlinck was a master at writing climaxes to his scenes.

The story of the play hinges on the activities of Tyltyl and Mytyl, the woodcutter's children who, in what ultimately proves to have been a dream, enter the realms of Fairyland on a quest for the Blue Bird of Happiness. After several abortive attempts to locate its position, the fairy known as Light (who guides them throughout their journey) suggests it might be hidden in a grave in a certain country churchyard. Maeterlinck's stage-directions for this scene are worth quoting:

> It is night. The moon is shining on a country churchyard. Numerous tombstones, grassy mounds, wooden crosses, stone slabs, etc. Tyltyl and Mytyl are standing by a short stone pillar.

By her very nature, Light may not accompany the children into the churchyard after dark. She therefore leaves them alone, having instructed Tyltyl to turn a magic diamond (he is wearing it in his little green cap) as soon as the church clock begins to strike the hour of midnight.

Mytyl is terrified. She admits as much to Tyltyl who, though he tries very hard to conceal the fact, is himself none too comfortable.

'Are the dead wicked?' asks Mytyl.

'Why, no', answers Tyltyl. 'They're not alive.'

'Have you ever seen one?'

'Yes, once—long ago, when I was very young.'

'What was it like?'

'Quite white, very still, and very cold. And it didn't talk.'

Mytyl, who is obviously getting more and more frightened every minute, continues to ask questions. Tyltyl does his best to answer her reassuringly, but even his gallantry suffers a decline as the hour of midnight approaches.

'When will you turn the diamond?' inquires Mytyl apprehensively.

'You heard Light say I was to wait until midnight.'

'Is it midnight yet?'

'Can't you see the church clock?'

'Yes; I can even see the small hand.'

'Midnight is just going to strike. . . . There! Do you hear?'

Mytyl screams.

'Tyltyl! I want to go away.'

'Not now. I am going to turn the diamond.'

'No, no, Tyltyl! Don't. I want to go away. I am terribly frightened.'

'But there is no danger, Mytyl.'

'I don't want to see the dead, Tyltyl. I don't want to see them.'

'Very well; you shan't see them. Shut your eyes.'

Mytyl is now trembling with terror. She clings to Tyltyl who is doing his best to be brave. He pulls himself together and stands erect. He is equally terrified, but he intends to be brave before his little sister. He raises his voice and says steadily:

'It is time . . . *THE HOUR IS PASSING*'. . .

He turns the diamond. In his simple action might well

lie the whole meaning of the difference between death and life. Perhaps that is all that really happens when the last moment of a human entity on earth is reached? Do Gabriel or Raphael or Michael turn a magic diamond? Something almost as simple must happen.

Here is Maeterlinck's next stage-direction:

> Tyltyl turns the diamond. A terrifying moment of silence and motionlessness elapses after which, slowly, the crosses totter, the mounds open, the slabs rise up.

'Tyltyl! They are coming out' . . .

> Then, from all the gaping tombs, there rises gradually an efflorescence—at first frail and timid, like steam; then white and virginal and more and more tufty, more and more tall and plentiful and marvellous. Little by little, irresistibly, invading all things, it transforms the graveyard into a sort of fairylike and nuptial garden over which rise the first rays of the dawn. The dew glitters; the flowers open their blooms; the wind murmurs in the trees; the bees hum; the birds wake and flood the first raptures of their hymns to the sun and to life. Stunned and dazzled, Tyltyl and Mytyl, holding each other by the hand, take a few steps among the flowers while they seek for a trace of the tombs.

And so they pass, or so it seems, from this world into the next. Gradually the sun rises, and the church bells ring out a welcome to them in their new life. They forget the dark and the cold they knew in the symbol of death, and laugh happily as they stoop to gather flowers that are growing in profusion all round them. Each is resolved to gather the bigger bunch to give to the fairy Light. How pleased she will be!

Suddenly Mytyl stops picking the blooms and gazes round her, evidently thinking. She ponders about those graves. They have gone; even the big one with the railing round it. Only a few minutes ago —or was it years ago?— she and Tyltyl were in the valley of the shadow of death. The dead were all round them.

Tyltyl is still busy picking flowers. Mytyl looks up at the church tower and listens to the bells. She then turns to her brother and calls him by name, but he has moved further away and is still bent on enlarging the handsome bunch he has already gathered.

'Tyltyl!' . . .

Still crouching, he glances up at her.

'Where are the dead, Tyltyl?'

Her question brings Tyltyl back to earth. He gets up and looks round him in a puzzled fashion. Then he slowly resumes his work without a word. But Mytyl, when she asks a question, requires an answer.

'Where are the dead?' she repeats.

Brave little philosopher Tyltyl! He does not even look round him again. Neither does it occur to him that he speaks a whole world of wisdom when he says—quite casually —over his shoulder:

'*There are no dead.*'

Every night I watched the effect of that line. When the lights went up there were very few dry eyes in that theatre.

Maeterlinck's thoughts embrace the whole meaning of life. There are no dead! Life is a going-on here until the Giver-of-life is good enough to turn Tyltyl's magic diamond. The valley of the shadow of death, represented by the graveyard with its tombs and crosses, becomes an enchanted garden with the bees humming and the bells ringing their changes—which mark the change-over from life into Life. Such a thought forbids—even ridicules—the morbidity of wearing black clothes; the change-over is a matter for congratulation, for saying 'good-bye—and good luck!' Any suggestion of the funereal is out-of-court, bad taste, irreverent, pagan. *It is much ado about nothing*: there is *no* death.

Who was it, do you suppose, who first thought of an angel of death? There are angels—legions of them—but there is no Angel of Death. You may remember that Jacob said a delightful thing while blessing his sons: 'The angel, which redeemed me from all evil, bless the lads!' Isaiah, in one of his most powerful prophecies, said: 'He was their Saviour. In all their affliction he was afflicted, and the angel of his presence saved them.' St John gives a pleasing account to the effect that 'an angel went down at a certain season into the pool, and troubled the water. Whosoever then first, after the troubling of the water, stepped in, was made whole of whatsoever disease he had.' St Paul spoke of Satan being transformed into an angel of light.

Very charming—all of it; but there is no Angel of Death. Angels, being messengers, are busy beings. The Angel of Death, if he existed, *would have nothing to do*.

John Bright allowed his imagination to run away with him when, in 1855, he said: 'The Angel of Death has been abroad throughout the land; you may almost hear the beating of his wings.' Perhaps it was the good John who invented the title?

So much has been written about death. It is quite diverting to examine some of it and try to sort it out. This is Matthew Arnold:

> And truly he who here
> Hath run his bright career,
> And served men nobly and acceptance found,
> And borne to light and right his witness high,
> What could he better wish than then to die
> And wait the issue, sleeping underground?

Beneke's ideas appear to evince a kind of hopeless cheerfulness :

> Why be heavy of heart, my brother;
> Why be weary or weep?
> For death ends all things, one with another,
> And death is a dreamless sleep.

Byron must have thought much the same:

> The silence of that dreamless sleep
> I envy now too much to weep.

Coleridge also:

> O what a wonder seems the fear of death
> Seeing how gladly we all sink to sleep!

This from Shakespeare :

> To sleep, perchance to dream;—ay, tnere's the rub;
> For in that sleep of death, what dreams may come
> When we have shuffled off this mortal coil?

Shakespeare at least has a notion that the so-called sleep of death may bring a dream or two along with it. He is a little more hopeful. For all that, he seems hazy as to his real feelings about death, according to this:

Ay, but to die, and go we know not where;
To lie in cold obstruction, and to rot;
This sensible warm motion to become
A kneaded clod; and the delighted spirit
To bathe in fiery floods, or to reside
In thrilling region of thick-ribbed ice;
To be imprisoned in the viewless winds,
And blown with restless violence round about
The pendent world.

Swinburne confesses his complete ignorance of death in:

Peace, rest, and sleep, are all we know of death,
And all we dream of comfort.

Beaumont and Fletcher, in their play *Thierry and Theodoret*, give a ghastly picture of death:

Endless parting
With all we can call ours, with all our sweetness,
With youth, strength, pleasure, people, time—nay, reason!
For in the silent grave no conversation,
No joyful tread of friends, no voice of lovers,
No careful father's counsels, things heard;
For nothing is, but all oblivion.

Campbell's prayer to Death:

O Death! If there be quiet in thy arms,
And I must cease—gently, O gently come
To me, and let my soul learn no alarms,
But strike me—ere a shriek can echo—dumb,
Senseless, and breathless.

This comment is Bishop Heber's, written after attending a funeral:

Death rides on every passing breeze,
He lurks in every flower;
Each season has its own disease.
Its perils every hour.

And Milton:

> Comes the blind Fury with the abhorrèd shears
> And slits the thin-spun life.

And he, who once signed his name in a hotel register as 'Percy Bysshe Shelley, *atheist*':

> How wonderful is Death,
> Death, and his brother Sleep!

I end with Plautus, who spoilt what might have been a great saying:

> He whom the gods love dies young, whilst he is full of health, perception, and judgement.

Plautus should have stopped at the first comma. Then he could have meant: he whom God loves dies young—young in heart, young in soul—no matter what age he may actually be. But there is no death; there are no dead. Tyltyl said so to Mytyl. And yet, every moment, humans are said to die. . . .

Or is it that they have just come to the end of all their thinking here? Is it just that the unfathomable, secret power (given them by the Creator at the beginning-of-things-here) has left them and sailed away into the sunset?

Yet, thinking of those who really do die young, it would seem that this cannot always be; for not all had time to do much thinking. Some never got so far as to do any at all.

And how many sailed away when life seemed so fresh and vivid, when all four winds blew nothing but good! How many sailed away in the early afternoon before there was time to finish their thinking! Why did they sail away so soon? Perhaps they were asked to leave their work here and begin other work over there, beyond the deepening clouds of evening?

Such secrets are not ours. We are not expected to spend time trying to fathom the unfathomable. Instead, as time goes on and we enter the period called *age*, we may find ourselves forgetting to look forward but, instead, remembering to look back. We may remember moments spent in lovely surroundings, or in absorbing the beauties of great pictures, great sculpture, great music; moments spent with those we loved most, or with those whose intellect we ha.

learned to revere; moments spent in the society of children.

Or, our thoughts may wander back to those really great moments of our own personal successes—moments when we chanced to be in splendid form, when we felt and looked our best; moments when we expressed our deepest thoughts perfectly, or had written something, said something, played something, sung something, *really well*; moments when our little world of friends realized we had not come among them for nothing, that our striving after power had not been in vain.

We may then mingle such thoughts with those of the future; so that, when at last the Sunset Gong for us does sound, there will be a completely tranquil mind—just a quiet joy. We may want to 'stay up a little longer' as we did when we were little; but if we really have had the best out of life we have nothing to fear. This, our one and only human existence, is merely an incident in time; and, as time itself is only an incident in eternity, we can afford to lift up our hearts. If we have used our power to think, if we have thought subjectively and objectively in order to advance sufficiently to think *projectively*, our hearts should be singing all the day long for very joy of having lived, of living now, and of being allowed to live *always*. Our peace of mind will then be the peace of the Mind of God Himself. Such peace passes our understanding here and hereafter. As for the simple change men have learned to call by the ugly name of Death, we shall find that it amounts to nothing more than what happened to Tyltyl and Mytyl.

We shall find that someone has turned a magic diamond. It will be a grand moment—the grandest we have ever known. We may remember that the graves and tombs and crosses tottered and crashed as the church clock struck the hour, but we shall know that they were only symbols bound up with an earthly body we are glad enough to have left behind. We shall be standing in the full sunlight of Life listening to the bells of welcome; we shall begin to pick the flowers of the future and gratefully breathe in the sweet summer breezes of the Planes of the Eternal. We shall then take a step forward, knowing that what we believed is true:

There are no dead.